A FIERY GUIDE TO 101 OF THE WORLD'S BEST SAUCES

HOT SAUCE

NEIL RIDLEY & DEAN HONER

Illustrations by Naomi Wilkinson

Hardie Grant

QUADRILLE

CONTENTS

PART 1

4	Introduction
5	How This Book Works
8	A Hot-Potted History
12	The Heart of the Heat
14	The Top 10 Peppers and Their Properties
17	How to Taste Hot Sauce... And Live to Tell the Tale
26	The Fire Eater's Recipes

PART 2

40	The Fire Eater's Hot 101
41	**North America**
80	**Caribbean & South America**
102	**Africa**
112	**Europe**
148	**Middle & Far East**
162	**Australasia**
170	The Fire Eater's Quick-Glance Guide
172	Burn After Reading
174	Acknowledgements
175	About the Authors

PART 1

INTRODUCTION

A (very) warm welcome, all you Chilli-Heads, Heat Seekers and fellow Fire Eaters!

We hope you're well and fired up for a spirited adventure into the wider world of hot sauce. We're delighted you have chosen this book as a way to further your exploration into what has become a huge global phenomenon, with thousands of hot sauce brands, styles and producers stretched all around the globe.

HOW THIS BOOK WORKS

What we aim to do is bring you a 'bird's-eye' view (see what we did there?) of 101 of our favourite sauces from nearly 50 countries. It includes some absolute classics, as well as a plethora of new and unusual sauces from smaller independent producers, hailing all the way from the US West Coast and Mexico, across the Caribbean, South America, Europe and Africa, ending up in Asia and Australasia.

Before that, we'll give you a hot-potted history of the humble origins of hot sauce, a guide to the peppers themselves – the real stars of the show – plus tips on making your own first hot sauce recipe. We'll also take a little look at the science behind why we all love getting royally burned!

We'll explore all the things you need to enjoy a hot sauce tasting session – including the necessary antidotes – alongside 10 mouthwatering food and drink recipes we've developed to highlight the various styles of hot sauce showcased in this book.

This book is about fun and flavour exploration, not just heat! We've tried to develop a clear way to review each sauce on as level a playing field as possible with the aim of inspiring you to try as many as you can. This isn't about which is best, or even which is hottest; it's about drawing on uplifting, cultural stories from the makers and finding out why they set out to develop their little bottles of joy. Each review includes the following sections:

Origin We've tried to bring you as broad a spread from around the globe as possible, with some well-known locations and a few surprising ones too!

Chilli Type Expect to find a wide array of different pepper types here: everything from the humble jalapeño, serrano, chipotle, habanero to the super-hots: bhut jolokia, moruga scorpion and the hellish carolina reaper.

Background Some info on the history of the sauce and the makers themselves. What drove them to take their path of fiery fun?

Tasting Notes Subjective, but hopefully informative, too. We'll give you the skinny on the key flavours present and just how, where and when the heat hits.

We've given each sauce a **Fire Eater's Rating,** based on our impression of its level of heat.

You'll also find one sauce that we deem beyond the realm of this rating as it's so utterly brutal on the palate!

Other Varieties to Seek Out Where applicable, you'll find a few other suggestions from the same maker also worth trying.

Use It For How to use each sauce is, of course, entirely up to you, but we offer a few suggestions you may like to try. Everything from scrambled eggs to ice cream!

Meet the 'Saucerers'...

Alongside the sauce reviews you'll find a few longer interviews with some truly inspiring people who have poured their hearts and souls into their recipes. Some you may have heard of, and a few are real mavericks of their craft. We've asked them to give their top expert tips on how to get the most out of your hot sauces as well as what inspired them to get creative in the first place.

So sit back, pour yourself something classy, and turn up the heat.

Let's burn, baby, burn.

Neil & Dean
@thefireeatersguide

PART 1

A HOT-POTTED HISTORY

6000 BC (or Birth of Chilli)

Given the hypothetical luxury of a time machine, a smartphone and a few modern-day hot sauces, it would be fascinating to set the destination to Central America around 6000 BC and capture the reaction of the ancient Mayans as they sampled a taste of what they were arguably responsible for helping to create. Would they recognize and enjoy the flavours, or would today's hot sauces be a step too far off the flavour map for them?

The Mayans of Mesoamerica – the region that extends from modern-day central Mexico, down through Central America and its surrounding islands to Costa Rica – are widely regarded as the first users of chilli peppers. Mayans likely domestically cultivated peppers, ripening, harvesting and grinding them down with water to create a crude but potentially potent chilli paste. This paste was used in a variety of dishes – as well as ceremonial drinks such as *cacahuatl*, a spiced, sweetened concoction that also included cocoa and vanilla beans that, in essence, was the original hot chocolate!

Archaeologists exploring cave sites in the Tehuacán Valley and Chiapa de Corzo in Mexico have unearthed evidence that the Mayans and Mixe-Zoquean-speaking cultures were spicing up their lives, finding traces of dihydrocapsaicin – a chemical similar to capsaicin, the all-important substance that gives chilli peppers their potency (see page 12). The Mayans' love of chilli peppers didn't just extend to culinary uses. Chillies were a thing of beauty, status, health and wealth. It is thought Mayans believed in both the healing properties and spiritual significance of the pepper, with chillies offered as tributes to deities and to people of status.

The European Chilli Explosion

The late 15th century was an important time for the chilli pepper as its popularity and fame grew across western Europe alongside a fascination for spices such as Indian long peppercorns, which had been teasing European palates since Roman times.

Christopher Columbus returned from the Americas and Caribbean with a cargo-load of goods, which he presented to Spain's royalty. In the space of a few years, the chilli plants began to be domestically cultivated and traded for great profit among wealthy and aristocratic families. The 16th century saw the heat spread into Eastern Europe via the Ottoman Empire, and paprika became a potent staple across Hungary and its surrounding regions, firing up pots of traditional goulash.

Sixteenth-century Portuguese explorers set their sights on Asia, taking the first chillies to the shores of Japan, Korea, Thailand and China, where the climatic conditions were perfect for growing chilli plants. These were soon bred to create more potent varieties, which had a considerable impact on the region's cuisine. India and Pakistan followed suit and the spice routes from Asia and India into the Mediterranean and North Africa became hugely lucrative for chilli growers, with both seeds and mature plants trading hands, expanding the number of varieties and styles.

The Birth of Hot Sauce as We Know and Love It

Just as the Mayans enjoyed their rudimentary chilli pastes, other cultures have created their own styles of sauces, which in turn have become hugely influential on today's modern hot sauce craze:

Korean Gochujang
A slightly fermented red chilli paste – check out CJ Haechandle.

Chinese Chilli Oil
Pungent dried chilli flakes in oil – for example, Lao Gan Ma.

Indonesian Sambal Oelek
A thick chilli sauce with vinegar, garlic and sometimes shrimp paste – check out Lucullus.

Ghanaian Shito
A fiery, dark and richly smoky condiment – check out Ghana Best or Ghana's Choice.

Middle Eastern Shatta
A paste based on red or green chillies, fermented in the sun – Ottolenghi makes a very good one.

Schug or Zhoug
Pronounced 'skoog', this is another Middle-Eastern spiced green sauce, which originated in Yemen – check out Belazu for a well-rounded version.

Peri Peri (or Piri Piri/Pili Pili)
A fragrant spicy and zesty sauce, originally from Africa but with a Portuguese influence, that historically uses the bird's eye chilli – see Maçarico, page 126.

Moroccan Harissa
A wonderfully dry and smoky chilli paste – see Le Phare du Cap Bon, page 110.

Biber Salçasi
A Turkish sauce with roasted puréed peppers, lemon juice and salt – check out Öncü.

Nam Phrik
A rich sauce from Thailand that uses chilli, garlic, lime juice, shallots and fish sauce – check out Maepranom.

Sriracha
Supposedly named after the Thai coastal town of Si Racha – see Shark, page 152.

Alongside these, the smoother, finer, more Western-style Louisiana 'dropping or dashing' sauce can trace its roots back to America at the start of the 19th century when cayenne sauce was advertised as both a condiment and medicinal tonic. Later that century producers such as J McCollick & Company began to create a sauce using the bird variety of pepper, which likely shared similarities with the modern pequin chilli. Then, in 1868, things got really spicy when Edward McIlhenny (see page 68) harvested his first crops of Louisiana-grown tabasco peppers and changed the culinary landscape forever with his now globally ubiquitous sauce of the same name.

Following in the footsteps of McIlhenny and his ground-breaking Tabasco sauce, other US-based brands such as New Orlean's Crystal (page 48) and Frank's (page 53), as well as Malaysia's Lingham's (see page 149) and Jamaica's Pickapeppa (page 97) have also recently celebrated centenaries, demonstrating the enduring love for recipes that use only a few simple ingredients and showcase the beauty and deeply radiant history of the chilli pepper.

In post-war America and Europe the influx of immigrants from the Caribbean, Asia and Africa created more diverse communities and gave rise to a demand for products with the 'flavours of home', especially in the form of condiments and hot sauces. Companies such as Encona (see page 81) endeavoured to bring a taste of Jamaica to the UK, while before that La Preferida (see page 60) had developed sauces and ingredients for the growing Mexican community in the US.

Rocket Fuel for Only the Bravest of Pilots!

The explosion of hot sauces in the modern era is nothing short of amazing. During the mid-1980s, David Tran introduced the UK, USA and Europe to his Huy Fong 'Rooster' Sriracha (page 58), a brand that would go on to spawn countless similar-looking, taste-alike sauces. In the 1990s pioneers such as Blair Lazar and Dave Hirschkop turned up the heat by releasing the first of a wave of extreme sauces such as Blair's Original Death Sauce (see page 42) and Dave's Gourmet Insanity Sauce (page 51). Peppers such as the habanero and scotch bonnet took centre stage and were revered for their punch and power.

As our palates adjusted to these blazing, fiery beasts, the types of pepper used in modern hot sauces developed (see our guide to some of the most popular peppers on page 14) and new breeds began to gain fearsome reputations for their incredible heat, as well as their unique flavours.

The Dawn of the 'Super Hots'

Pepper-growing legends such as Frank Garcia, Paul Bosland of the Chile Pepper Institute in New Mexico, and later Smokin' Ed Currie (see page 15) put their devilish minds to work to engineer fruit that would shatter the supposed ceiling of the Scoville heat scale for spiciness (see page 13), introducing the likes of the red savina, the bhut jolokia (or ghost pepper) the moruga scorpion and the infamous, current Guinness World Record holder, the carolina reaper, to modern day sauces. The touch paper had been well and truly lit and the world of hot sauce went stratospheric!

Today the global hot sauce business has been joined by thousands of new players and flavour explorers, some from culinary backgrounds (see Maison Martin, page 133), others from horticultural ones (see Wiltshire Chilli, page 143, and PuckerButt, page 61), and others, well... they're just creating their own sauce identities for the sheer hell of pushing the boundaries of how hot is 'too hot'!

Elsewhere, other producers are experimenting with additional ingredients, such as beer and spirits (see Raijmakers, page 135, and Thiccc, page 144), with complex blends of different pepper flavours (see Khoo's Sauces, page 127), while some are considering the wider community and 'terroir' aspects of growing peppers for the sauces they make (see Small Axe Peppers, page 69). There's also a trend towards sweeter, more 'dessert-led' sauces, indulging our love of chocolate, cherries and, now, pepper-infused 'hot honey' (see Chorrito, page 114).

Something tells us the Mayans would be impressed with how far things have come – and a little proud of how the global palate has warmed to their pungent, peppery delights.

THE HEART OF THE HEAT

*Taking a closer look at the peppers
that tantalize our tongues.*

Peppers are remarkable constructions. With so many distinctive colours, shapes and levels of potency, they have an allure like no other fruiting plant. They belong to the *Capsicum* genus, part of the nightshade family of plants, which also includes tomatoes and the humble potato. But what marks peppers out is capsaicin, the powerful alkaloid compound inside them that is particularly concentrated in the white, pithy strands in the pod around the seeds.

Capsaicin is a brilliantly 'designed', but ultimately fatally flawed, defence mechanism. It's there to stop the peppers being eaten by triggering a burning sensation, which particularly affects mammals. But while the chilli gods failed to anticipate our penchant for ritually grilling our palates, they did have the foresight to render birds more or less immune to its effects, allowing them to happily eat the pods and then distribute the seeds whenever they need a 'comfort break'.

Today the business of cultivating peppers is incredibly broad, with as many as 3,000 different varieties grown around the world. However – and this may sound surprising – all these are the descendants or cultivars of just five domesticated varieties:

Capsicum annuum
from which the jalapeño and cayenne originate

Capsicum frutescens
which includes the tabasco and piri piri

Capsicum chinense
which includes the habanero, scotch bonnet and naga

Capsicum pubescens
which includes the distinct-tasting rocoto, see page 132

Capsicum baccatum
which includes the amarillo and lemon drop varieties

The Scoville Scale:
The Numerical Stairway to Hell

For over a hundred years the Scoville Scale has determined how pepper growers, sauce makers and legions of obsessed chilli-heads rank the intensity of the experience of a chilli pepper. The system was devised by American pharmacist Wilbur Scoville back in 1912, who added a precise weight of dried chilli to an alcohol solution to liberate the capsaicinoids present in the pepper. He then reduced the solution using varying, precisely measured amounts of water until an expert panel of five tasters could no longer detect the capsaicin's presence or burning effect.

The result is measured in **Scoville Heat Units (SHU)** and is given as a sliding scale – with a minimum and maximum to be expected – in order to account for the subjectivity of the tasters' tolerance and the natural flaws in each pepper type (i.e. the fact that different growing locations often lead to differing intensities of heat).

The system to gauge SHU has been improved for consistency in recent times and now uses modern liquid chromatography, which allows the capsaicin to be scientifically measured in parts per million. This result is then multiplied by 16 to give the official Scoville Heat Rating.

Fun Fact

Pure, unadulterated capsaicin extract measures 16 million Scoville Heat Units. The humble bell pepper measures zero, while even pepper spray used by the police has a rating, rocking in at 5.3 million SHU!

It begs the question: how do you apply for a job on the Scoville panel? You don't have to be hot-headed to work here... but it helps!

THE TOP 10 PEPPERS AND THEIR PROPERTIES

Let's look at what might be considered the top 10 chillies used in today's sauces: from mild peppers to the hottest of the super hots.

Jalapeño
2,500–8,000 SHU (Mexico)

One of the most popular peppers in the world, the jalapeño can trace its roots to the Mexican town of Xalapa (Jalapa) and parts of Central America. It has a fresh, crisp vegetal flavour, with a slightly herbaceous note. Both Texas and California are the leading growing locations of this versatile pepper, which is used in both its unripened green and fully ripened red forms. The chipotle pepper is a dried, smoked variation of the jalapeño.

Serrano
10,000–25,000 SHU (Mexico)

Another legendary Mexican pepper. Its name means 'from the mountain', which is fitting, given it originates from the mountainous regions of Mexico's Puebla and Hidalgo states. Thinner than the jalapeño, the serrano tends to have a slightly bitter flavour, with some zesty citrus notes.

Cayenne
30,000–50,000 SHU (French Guyana)

This popular scorcher is a kitchen staple in its powdered form and a favourite in plenty of classic sauces (see Frank's, page 53, and Crystal, page 48). It's thought to have originated in French Guyana and was spread to the rest of the world by 16th-century Portuguese spice traders. Today its major areas of growth include Africa, India, Mexico and Japan, as well as the USA.

Habanero
100,000–350,000 SHU (South America)

This ancient pepper was first discovered over 8,000 years ago around the Amazon in South America. Its name comes from the Spanish for Havana, as it was a popular and highly-prized pepper traded around the Cuban capital, despite not playing much of a role in Cuban cuisine. Now prevalent in the Yucatán area of Mexico, the 'hab' is a hot-sauce staple, with a steadily rising heat. It's often used when red and ripe, although there are a number of alternative versions, including orange and darker chocolate varieties that have a richer, more pungent taste and heat.

Scotch Bonnet
100,000–350,000 SHU (Caribbean)

A distant relative of the habanero, the scotch bonnet is part of the *Capsicum chinense* family. This small, squat pepper owes its name to its resemblance to a classic Scottish tam o' shanter hat. A key part of Caribbean cooking, especially in Jamaica, Barbados and St Lucia, it is fresh and fruity, with a pungent, swift, biting heat. Scotch bonnets are used in an array of different hues: from yellow and the more commonly used ripe orange, to bright red and occasionally a darker chocolate variety.

African Bird's Eye
175,000–200,000 SHU (Mexico)

Despite its name, this pepper is another Mexican original but, like many others, became a stalwart across Africa after arriving via 16th-century spice traders. Now its heartland lies in Malawi, but it also enjoys great degrees of success in Ghana, Zimbabwe, Kenya, Eswatini and South Africa. For a small, thin pepper, it has a devilish, dry, biting heat and a little goes a long way.

Bhut Jolokia/Ghost Pepper
800,000–1,041,427 (India)

Back in 2006, this north-east Indian beast was the certified hottest pepper on the planet. The pepper gets its spooky reputation – *bhut* means 'ghost' in the Assam region of India – from the fact that it comes in a striking white version (as well as the more common orange). The flavour is wonderfully fresh and fruity, with a sweet citrus note. The heat also rises very slowly into a blistering intensity, with a hugely lengthy finish.

Naga Viper
900,000–1,382,118 SHU (UK)

A triple-threat pepper and make no mistake! Created by British grower Gerald Fowler, it combines properties of the naga morich (from Bangladesh), the bhut jolokia and the Trinidad scorpion. This super-hot chilli brings a distinct fruity note, with a woody, smoky undertone and is, of course, insanely powerful.

Moruga Scorpion
1,200,000–2,000,000 SHU (Trinidad)

The sting in the tail is all too real with this terrifying chilli. First cultivated in Trinidad and Tobago by farmer Wahid Ogeer, this lantern-shaped pepper has a pronounced point or 'sting' and wrinkled skin, and delivers an almost pleasant, stone/tropical fruit flavour with a herbaceous backbone before the unrelenting burn begins. Brutal, but absolutely magic in the right sauces.

Carolina Reaper
1,400,000–2,200,000 SHU (USA)

King of the Hill, A-number one… the giant-slaying carolina reaper has swung its merciless scythe to officially claim its place – at the time of writing – as the world's hottest pepper. Its creator, Puckerbutt's Smokin' Ed Currie cross-bred a Pakistani naga and a red habanero from St Vincent to create this wrinkly, yet surprisingly sweet fruity hellhound. For the last decade, the Reaper has come to define the final frontier in extreme heat and, in turn, has revolutionized the world of hot sauce. However, Mr Currie's recent experiments with new creations 'Pepper X' and 'Apollo' (see page 56) look set to eclipse this masterwork.

Other notable peppers to look out for . . .

Ancho
1,000–1,500 SHU
When dried, this is one of the key ingredients in classic Mexican mole sauce.

Arbol
15,000–30,000 SHU
A small, bright red pepper and a fine choice for mild-medium heat applications and particularly good in a spicy Mexican-style hot chocolate.

Tabasco
30,000–50,000 SHU
The pepper that's given its name to the ubiquitous sauce!

Madame Jeanette
100,000–350,000 SHU
An attractive, curvaceous yellow pepper from Suriname, with plenty of feistiness.

Fatalii
125,000–400,000 SHU
An unusual central African delight and a pepper with a unique, citrus-led flavour and plenty of heat.

Red Savina
200,000–577,000 SHU
A frighteningly hot take on the red habanero, which crops up in sauces now and again.

7-Pot Douglah
923,889–1,853,986 SHU
So named because just one pepper can supposedly spice up to seven big pots of stew!

Dragon's Breath
2,480,000 SHU (unofficial)
A UK-bred pepper that, at the time of writing, is (unofficially) hotter than the carolina reaper! Let's call this an Ultra Hot.

Pepper X
3,180,000 SHU (unofficial)
Another unofficial Ultra Hot by the same twisted mind that brought the carolina reaper into the world. Also see the Apollo on page 56.

HOW TO TASTE HOT SAUCE ...
AND LIVE TO TELL THE TALE

Our infatuation with hot sauces is most closely linked to the joy of discovering their extraordinary array of flavours and the thrill of experiencing the glorious, rising warmth – and sometimes brutal bite – that comes with the most pungent of peppers used in the recipes. So, what's the best way to approach tasting of a range of hot sauces – and what are the key things to look out for?

Over the next few pages we'll lay out our guide to building a solid collection of hot sauces, exploring the different groups of flavours within them, and suggesting some outstanding food styles and recipes to try with each one. We'll also look at what remedies to turn to when you need to hit the ejector seat button away from the heat! Think of it as the ultimate hot-sauce taster's antidote kit...

Our Love Affair with Pain and Pleasure

The science behind the way we enjoy the perception of heat in food is a complicated business, but it all comes down to a fine chemical-versus-hormonal balancing act, where the battleground is our mouth.

The capsaicin found in chilli peppers affects certain receptors in our body – especially in the mouth and on the tongue – known as TRPV1, or Trip-Vee-One receptors, which are responsible for registering the threat of extreme heat (they also respond to fresh ginger, wasabi and black pepper). This effectively triggers a distress call to the brain saying that our mouth is on fire and in immediate need of an extinguisher!

Our body then deploys its emergency response 'task force' – a combination of adrenaline, dopamine, serotonin and norepinephrine – which raises the heart rate, causes us to sweat and shake, makes our nose run (to help rid the body of the flames), and then leaves us with a sense of euphoria once the burn has subsided. In many respects, this is not dissimilar to the thrill we experience when we throw ourselves out of a plane: the body's natural reaction to such obvious danger is 'are you absolutely mad?', but the payoff is certainly worth the effort...

So, if you wanna feel the high, something's gotta fry!

The 'Classic' Hot Sauce Styles for Your Collection

As we explored earlier, hot sauce has over the centuries grown into a globally adored culture within cuisine, with a number of styles and heat levels, each one influenced by where and by whom it is made. While there are countless varieties, from Turkish biber salçasi, to Korean gochujang paste, to Yemeni zhoug, we've tried to bring together a group of six, easily accessible, essential sauce styles that make a great starting point for your collection. These are by no means the only bottles you'll ever need, but they provide a broad spectrum of flavours and offer boundless culinary versatility. There are many hybrids that straddle a few of these different flavour camps too.

Louisiana Style These fine-consistency 'dashing' sauces are largely influenced by the likes of Tabasco (see page 68), Frank's (page 53) and Crystal (page 48) and often bring together a 'mash' of simple ingredients, including cayenne pepper, vinegar, sugar and salt. Many Louisiana sauces are fermented and aged in containers – sometimes for several years – before they are blended and bottled to develop their distinct piquant, savoury characters.

Flavour characteristics to look out for:
Saline/Dry/Sour/Fermented/Citrus

Mexican Picante Style – Green and Red Two very distinct styles, but both absolutely essential. Mexico has a hugely textured history with hot sauce, and the darker, richer, more complex 'red' sauces, such as Cholula (page 46) and Valentina Salsa Picante (page 72), are wonderful everyday sauces for spicing up enchiladas, beef tacos or huevos rancheros. Equally important are the 'verde' green styles made from fresh, herbaceous, vegetal green jalapeño, habanero and other peppers, such as El Yucateco (page 79), Amazon Pepper Co's Green Amazon sauce (page 80), and Maratá Gota Picante Molho de Pimenta Verde (page 88). These offer a real refreshing contrast, which is perfect for eggs or light fish dishes.

Flavour characteristics to look out for:
Red: Dry/Spicy/Meaty/Fruity

Green: Herbaceous/Vegetal/Saline/Citrus

Sriracha Style These Asian-influenced, spicy, rich and often garlic-heavy sauces are known for their silky, sticky-sweet consistency and deep flavour. Sriracha originated in south-east Asia and has subsequently taken the world by storm with its rich and powerful character and distinct heat, which is perfect for noodle and stir-fry dishes. Notable classics include Huy Fong (page 58) and Shark (page 152), and for more modern takes on Sriracha, check out the versions by Yellowbird (page 77) and Thiccc (page 144).

Flavour characteristics to look out for:
Sweet/Fruity/Spicy/Oniony

Caribbean Style The hot sauces of the Caribbean (particularly Barbados and Jamaica) are among some of the most influential in the world and many have the distinct citrussy, aromatic heat of the scotch bonnet pepper at their heart. Some often have sweeter, more perfumed notes, including tropical fruit, alongside heavier, hotter mustard flavours and aromas. Great authentic examples include Aunt May's (page 83), Baron (page 84), Matouk's (page 89), and Dirty Dick's (page 45).

Flavour characteristics to look out for:
Fruity/Floral/Oniony/Citrus/Spicy

Chipotle Style Distinct, dry and smoky, chipotle sauces are often made using dried, smoked, jalapeño peppers and have a wonderful, warming, well-rounded and beautifully roasted note to them – a perfect pairing for barbecued meat and other more robust flavours. Check out Condimaniac Smokey Dragon (page 112).

Flavour characteristics to look out for:
Smoky/Spicy/Dry/Meaty

Other Additions Next to these more 'classic' styles, it's worth considering a few signature ingredient sauces, such as roasted garlic-led expressions or more fruit-driven concoctions featuring mango, papaya or pineapple (see La Meridana on page 60 or Heriot Hott on page 124), which are wonderful for pepping up salads and fresh salsas.

Finally, there's always shelf space for something a little 'wild card'... and the sky's the limit there!

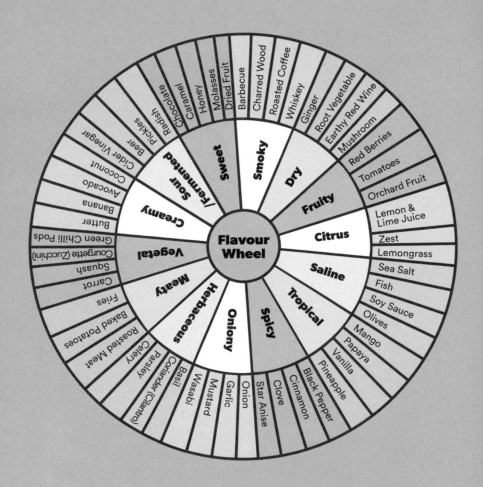

Writing Hot Sauce Tasting Notes

Think of the experience of tasting hot sauce as a journey, or an adventure. How do you expect it to start? Where could the flavours take you? How long will the heat last? When will the burn properly bite? And which flavours are you left tasting after the adventure has ended?

It's worth grabbing a notebook to record your findings, breaking the experience down into several stages:

1. The Initial Aromas

What do you get straight out of the bottle when you remove the lid? A waft of fresh, fruity pepper? A burst of something sharp, like lemon zest? Or maybe a drier, more complex spiciness?

2. Consistency & Thickness

What consistency is the sauce? Fine and runny? Or do you have to slap the bottom of the bottle to get any out? What texture is it? Smooth, silky and creamy, or more coarse, fleshy and seed-heavy?

3. That First Taste

Taking a teaspoon, or using a small wooden tasting stick (highly recommended), add a small amount to the middle of the tongue. What are the initial flavours? Do they tally with the list of ingredients on the back label? What is the lead 'signature' flavour? Can you also identify the flavours and style of the pepper used? (For suggestions, see our pepper properties section on pages 14–16.)

4. The Balancing Act

Try a slighter larger amount this time, now your palate has got used to the flavour and heat. Does everything taste nicely balanced, or is anything too dominant or weak? Is it too sweet, salty or vinegar-led?

5. The Finish

Which flavours linger in the mouth – and for how long? Is it a lingering dry flavour, something sweeter, or more savoury?

6. How Hot Is It?

Super subjective, given everyone has a different tolerance to hot flavours, but try to rank each sauce on an initial one-to-five scale (with one being mildest and five the most smoking hot). You can always go back and review your scores once you've tasted more.

The Heatwave – All the Same? Think Again...

The way that peppers convey heat into a hot sauce is an intriguing thing indeed. While we have tried to give each sauce tasted in this book a **Fire Eater's Rating** on a scale of one to five to indicate its heat intensity (one being mild and five being exceptionally hot), it's also worthwhile considering how *quickly* the heat arrives, when its most *intense* moment hits and how slowly it *dissipates*. Remember: heat levels are subjective – one taster's tolerance is different from another's, so bear that in mind with any ratings on the bottle label. If you're tasting a range of sauces, work up to the hottest one, rather than diving straight in feet first: it will undoubtedly improve your experience of the more flavoursome, subtler, milder ones!

Some peppers deliver a fresh, fruity note upfront with the heat only arriving slowly to give a long sustained burn. Others inflict an immediate, sharp attack of sizzling, dry heat that fades quickly. Time the length and record your thoughts!

Think of it like a musical note, with an **Attack, Sustain and Release**.

The Hot Sauce Taster's Emergency Kit

Whatever your tolerance for heat, you'll inevitably find your limit at some point – the culinary equivalent of hanging off a cliff face by your fingernails, a rapidly rising inferno waiting to engulf you below. Some say this is all part of what makes hot sauce such a wonderfully fun and unique phenomenon – UK hot-sauce producer Liam Kirwan of Manchester's Devil Dog (see page 119) puts it brilliantly bluntly:

'Don't come to the rodeo if you're not prepared to ride the bull!'

But should you find yourself at that fiery precipice, help is at hand.

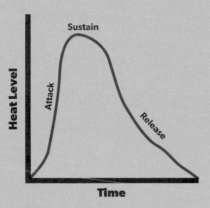

Heat Level

Sustain

Attack

Release

Time

While the knee-jerk reaction is to reach for the nearest glass of water or cold beer, these liquids are very much unhelpful. All you'll succeed in doing is washing the heat further around your mouth and into awaiting pain receptors, as capsaicin isn't soluble in water. There are a few other things that do work, however. They'll not only help to dissipate and break down the capsaicin, but also to rapidly cool your mouth.

To test them, we put ourselves right in the 'fire-ing' line. Armed with a bottle of Heatonist's Apollo (a stupendously brutal yet flavoursome hot sauce, see page 56) and a fresh moruga scorpion pepper, we set out to prove and disprove which of the most common remedies against pepper heat are the most effective, ranking them out of 10. It wasn't pretty, but somebody had to do it...

Hot Sauce Tasting Tips

Never eat Super Hot sauces on an empty stomach. Always try to prepare yourself by eating some thick yogurt or a milky dish, such as rice pudding – it really makes a difference in warding off any cramps you might experience!

If you want to refresh your palate between sauces, try eating a dry cracker.

Some smaller artisanal hot sauces may not contain preservatives, so refrigerate any bottles to keep them as fresh and zingy as the day you first opened them. Both sunlight and heat can adversely affect the 'brightness' of flavours.

Dairy-Based Remedies

Milk Refreshing and cooling, milk provides an admirable, but not exactly perfect, antidote. If you don't like drinking milk, try a milkshake instead.

6/10

Mango lassi Very effective at instantly quelling the burn. Needs a second mouthful to bring the heat under control, but the combo of dairy and sweetness works fantastically well to dampen the flames.

8/10

Kefir Instantaneous relief, but the burn soon returns.

5/10

Yogurt Full-fat Greek yogurt is thick and coating, giving immediate relief. Slight return. A stout defence!

8/10

Soft cheese Full-fat soft cheese is very effective – thick and tongue-coating. Only a slight return of the burn.

6/10

Mozzarella Buffalo milk contains a high amount of the protein casein, which dissipates capsaicin. It works extremely well indeed. Moo!

8/10

Rice pudding Creamy and cooling in the mouth. It is also a good tip to have some at the start of a tasting, to line the stomach.

6/10

Ice cream Full-fat dairy ice cream was mouth-coating and instantly cooling. Plus the sweetness really took the edge off the dry punch of the chilli. Our favourite remedy. Just choose a neutral flavour, like vanilla.

9/10

Sugar/Sweet-Based Remedies

Fruit gums/soft chewy candy
Sugar has been shown to help reduce the burn of chilli but these didn't help one bit!

1/10

Chocolate A milk-heavy variety helped to coat the palate and offered initial resistance and relief to the burn, but lacked long-term refreshment.

5/10

Fudge A real revelation! The combination of sweetness and dairy cream was immediately effective and coating, with only a slight heat return. It seemed to soften a particularly sharp burn too.

8/10

Sugary drink Still, cloudy lemonade was immediately quenching and cooling but didn't stop the burn washing around the mouth. Not 100% effective. Good for refreshing the palate at the end of a tasting.

5/10

Sugar, jam (jelly) and honey
Disappointing – the cloying sugariness only seemed to heighten the burn. Ouch!

2/10

Acidic-Based Remedies

Lemon/lime juice Freshly squeezed citrus juice is proven to help break down capsaicin, but it is only slightly effective here and the resulting mouthfeel and aftertaste aren't pleasant. Cooking hack: adding lemon quarters to an over-spicy stew or chilli during cooking does seem to bring the heat down somewhat. **4/10**

Vegan/Veggie Alternatives

Peanut butter/olive oil The fattiness seems to slowly help dull the burn. It returns, but perhaps not quite as intensively. **5/10**

Coconut milk/yogurt Cooling, but not as lingering and ultimately effective as the dairy-based versions. **3/10**

Avocado Offers a slightly cooling sensation. Maybe a little effective, but only temporarily. **3/10**

Cucumber Initially cooling but ultimately ineffective. **2/10**

Tomatoes and tomato juice Works on the upfront burn, but wateriness doesn't help in the long run. **4/10**

Alcohol

Neat vodka/whiskey/rum Not entirely sure about this one but it is certainly fun to try... **?/10**

THE FIRE EATER'S RECIPES

So many wonderful sauces out there... but how to use them?

We've whipped up a collection of easy-to-make food and drink recipes that work with a wide variety of different sauces. In each case, we've suggested our favourite sauces to try them with – some of them classics – but have a go at creating your own pairings too.

MAKING YOUR OWN HOT SAUCE

Some of the greatest, most enduring hot sauces have come from resurrected family recipes. Others are the result of tireless trial and error or, conversely, happy accidents that just worked out perfectly. If you've already got a taste for the stuff, why not have a go at creating your own? We asked some of the brightest minds and creators in the hot sauce community for their hints and tips for cooking up the next masterpiece.

Start Simple, Dream Big...

According to Hatsadee 'Yoyo' Xayavongchanch, creator of Yoyo Laos Sauce (page 158): 'Some hot sauces are very complex, using lots of ingredients, which don't necessarily mean a nicer sauce. Keep it simple, experiment – find out what works and what doesn't. Use the freshest ingredients and test it with as many people as you can: feedback is so valuable.'

Only Use Quality Ingredients...

'The key to many a great sauce is quality,' points out Dutch sauce maker Freek Raijmakers of Raijmakers Heetmakers (see page 135). 'Not only fresh peppers, but also the other ingredients should be of high quality. Take vinegar, for example. There are many types of vinegar and some are of very poor quality. Put that in a hot sauce and you'll ruin it.'

Develop a Signature Style...

Erica Diehl, founder of Queen Majesty Hot Sauce in New York (page 64), thinks originality is key: 'Stay very true to what YOU want out of a hot sauce, and don't try to copy someone else.'

Make a 'Base Batch' First...

Liam Kerr from Scotland's Heriot Hott (see page 124) says: 'Make a decent-sized batch of base ingredients [the chilli 'mash', usually using peppers, vinegar, salt and sugar] and then you can use this to control the heat profile. Divvy it up into smaller batches and you can start to use different amounts of additional ingredients to fine tune. For instance, 5% roasted garlic might be too much and would ruin the whole batch, so it's about controlling the flavours. But above all, have fun!'

Focus on Your Balance of Headline Flavours...

Clint Meyer, founder of Fire Dragon Chillies in New Zealand (page 164), recommends to 'get a good selection of chillies and try mixing them with organic cider vinegar, onion, garlic, lemon and lime juice and something to bulk it up – either fruit, carrot, capsicum or tomatoes work well. Once you get the basic sauces perfected, you can try some more complicated recipes.'

Don't Be Afraid to Experiment...

Some combinations might seem unusual but bring out the best in each other. Sweet and savoury combos also really tantalize the palate. Chocolate, cherry, roasted pineapple, agave nectar, gin, tequila, beer and truffle all feature in sauces mentioned in this book.

Don't Forget the *Flavour* of the Pepper, Not Just the Heat...

'I use a blend of chillies in my sauces – and the pepper flavour is very important to me,' says Rob Fletcher, founder of Dr Trouble in Zimbabwe (see page 107). 'I blend in cherry peppers to add some natural sweetness without much heat. Then there's African bird's eye also, which I use to balance the heat. In some flavours I use red demon chillies, to add some fruity flavour along with a strong heat.'

The Burning Question: How Hot Is TOO Hot?

Never forget that your own tolerance might be higher than others'. It's easier to add more heat than to take it out of a recipe, so start light and build up to the level you feel comfortable with... and get feedback! 'Select the heat level you are after first, then select the pepper that works for that heat level,' explains Erica Diehl. 'Once you select that pepper, you can consider its flavour too and build the other ingredients around it.'

Essential Tools for the Job

- Accurate digital kitchen scales

- Large, stainless steel pan for cooking your sauce batch

- Food processor (or, better still, a powerful hand blender) – something to give you the balance between a smooth consistency and a little texture from the chilli pods

- Sterilized screw-top glass bottles or jar

- A large sieve

- A funnel

- Latex gloves and eye protection – this might seem like total overkill, but trust us, if you're using any Super Hot variety of pepper, such as a reaper or scorpion, it's easy to transfer the pepper juice to your eyes AND other sensitive parts of the body. And you really don't want that to happen!

BASIC RED PEPPER SAUCE RECIPE

Makes around 350ml (1½ cups)

For a reasonably hot sauce, work on a two-to-one ratio of sweeter peppers to hot ones. Start with around 25g (1oz) of red habaneros or scotch bonnets as a good base to 50g (2oz) of sweet peppers, such as ramiro. For hotter recipes, explore switching out individual peppers for more fiery varieties. Remember, a little goes a long way!

Ingredients

2 tbsp olive oil
25g (1oz) red habanero or
    scotch bonnet peppers,
    stems removed and
    roughly chopped
50g (2oz) sweet peppers (such
    as ramiro), stems removed
    and roughly chopped
1 medium red onion (around
    150g/5½oz), finely chopped
2 fresh garlic cloves, minced
1 small/medium carrot (around
    60g/2¼oz), peeled and diced
100ml (½ cup) cider vinegar
5 fresh medium-sized tomatoes
    (around 130g/4½oz), diced
2–3 tsp salt
2 tsp sugar
1 tsp allspice

Method

Add the oil to a medium-sized saucepan and gently fry the peppers, onion, garlic and carrot until soft (being careful not to burn) for about 5–6 minutes over a medium heat, adding the vinegar halfway through. Reduce the heat and add the tomatoes, salt, sugar and allspice and slowly cook the mixture down for 7–10 minutes until slightly reduced.

Remove from the heat, pour into a blender (or jug/pitcher, if using a hand blender) and blitz until smooth. For a finely textured sauce, strain through a sieve into a bowl. Allow to cool before bottling.

HUEVOS RANCHEROS

Serves 1

This classic and utterly delicious brunch is fresh, herbaceous and wonderfully spicy, as well as super simple to make.

Fire Eater's Sauce Recommendation: Valentina Salsa Muy Picante (page 72) or Tapatío Salsa Picante (page 61)

Ingredients

1 soft corn tortilla
1 large tomato, diced
1 green jalapeño, sliced
½ handful fresh flat-leaf parsley, finely chopped
1 handful coriander (cilantro), finely chopped
1 fresh lime, juiced
1 tbsp olive oil
⅓ × 435g (15oz) can refried beans or 85g (½ cup) black beans
2 medium eggs (we like Burford Browns)
½ tbsp Valentina Salsa Muy Picante or Tapatío Salsa Picante hot sauce
Salt and freshly ground black pepper

Method

Lightly toast the tortilla in a dry pan until it has browned slightly.

Add the tomato to a bowl with the fresh jalapeño, parsley and coriander (cilantro). Add half the lime juice, plus the olive oil, into the bowl and season with salt and pepper. Mix thoroughly.

In a small pan add the refried/black beans and the rest of the lime juice and heat through, stirring occasionally.

Next, fry the eggs in a little olive oil or butter until browned and crispy at the edges.

Evenly spread the beans onto the tortilla, add the fresh tomato and herb mix and gently lay the eggs on top. Season with a little more cracked black pepper and a drizzle of the Valentina or a generous few dashes of the Tapatío.

DEVILLED LOBSTER ON TOAST

Serves 2

A devilishly simple, fun and wonderfully punchy brunch that really brings out the sweetness of the lobster and the warming bite of your favourite hot sauce.

Fire Eater's Sauce Recommendation: Secret Aardvark Serrabanero green sauce (page 67) or any other green jalapeño/serrano/habanero-based sauce for a distinct, fresh, herbaceous flavour

Ingredients

For the toast
½ a ripened, medium-sized avocado
Squeeze of fresh lime
2 medium-cut slices of sourdough bread
1 small garlic clove
Drizzle of olive oil
Salt and freshly ground black pepper

For the lobster tails
½ tsp cayenne pepper
Small piece of ground ginger, finely chopped
1 tbsp runny honey
1 tbsp soy sauce
2 tsp sun-dried tomato paste
Squeeze of fresh lemon juice
6 dashes green hot sauce
2 fresh, pre-cooked lobster tails, washed and shelled, slightly scored down the length
50g (1¾oz) unsalted butter
1 tbsp fresh coriander (cilantro), chopped
1 tbsp dry vermouth (optional)
Pinch of course ground sea salt

Method

Mash the avocado with a fork into a rough consistency, adding the lime juice and a pinch of salt and pepper. Under a medium grill (broiler), toast the sourdough, then score the garlic clove and gently rub over one side. Drizzle with olive oil and thickly spread the avocado on the toast.

Mix together the cayenne pepper, ginger, honey, soy sauce, tomato paste, lemon juice and hot sauce in a small bowl. Dip each lobster tail in the mixture until generously covered. In a medium-sized pan, melt the unsalted butter and sear the tails until golden for 4–5 minutes, adding the remainder of the marinade and the chopped coriander (cilantro) halfway through. If using, add the vermouth to the pan about a minute before the end. Remove from the heat and sprinkle the tails with sea salt.

Assemble the seared lobster tails over the top of the avocado toast. Finish off with an extra squeeze of lemon juice.

FIRECRACKER MARGARITA

Serves 1

One of the truly great classic cocktails, the Margarita brings together herbaceous notes of silver tequila and zesty lime juice for the perfect refreshing summer sipper. Add a little fresh chilli – and a couple of dashes of your favourite hot sauce – and this versatile, balanced beauty becomes the devil-in-disguise, ready to poke your taste buds with its forked tail!

Fire Eater's Sauce Recommendation: Howler Monkey Original (page 52) or Marie Sharp's Green Habanero (page 90)

Ingredients

50ml (2oz) silver tequila (Patrón Silver is ideal)
25ml (1oz) lime juice
25ml (1oz) triple sec
12ml (½oz) sugar syrup
2 dashes of hot sauce (or a third, if you dare...)
Slice of fresh lime
2 small red chillies (bird's eye or cayenne)

Method

Add all the ingredients (except the lime slice and chillies) into a cocktail shaker with ice and shake for 10–12 seconds, before pouring into an ice-filled tumbler glass.

Garnish with the slice of lime and assemble the chillies as devil horns to complete the look!

KILLER BLOODY MARIA

Serves 1 (with leftover Ultimate Searing Seasoning)

The Bloody Mary is one of the most iconic cocktails in the world. But if you fancy trying a slightly more savoury version, look no further than the Bloody Maria. Instead of vodka, this brunch classic uses silver or blanco tequila, which brings a wonderful herbaceous flavour to truly die for.

Fire Eater's Sauce Recommendation: Cholula (page 46)

Ingredients

For the Ultimate Searing Seasoning
2 tsp ground black pepper
1 tsp cayenne pepper
½ tsp ground allspice
2 tsp celery salt
½ tsp garlic powder
1 tsp horseradish
2 stock (bouillon) cubes, crumbled (beef or vegetable)
2 tbsp Worcestershire sauce
1 tbsp pickle juice (from a jar of cornichons or similar)
1 tbsp fresh lime juice
12 good dashes Cholula hot sauce

For the cocktail
50ml (2oz) silver tequila (such as Altos or 1800)
2 tsp sun-dried tomato paste
150ml (6oz) quality tomato juice
Cherry tomatoes, fresh lemon wedge and celery stick, to garnish

Method

Mix the seasoning ingredients well in a small jug (pitcher) and leave for 15 minutes. You can then store the mixture in a small sterilized dropper/dasher-style bottle and add it to each drink to deliver the ultimate bespoke mix of heat and savoury punch. Kept refrigerated, it should last for up to 2 months.

Add all the cocktail ingredients (except the garnishes) into a shaker and dry-shake (without ice) for 10 seconds to aerate the mixture. Fill a tall glass with ice and strain the drink into the glass. Add 5–10 drops of the seasoning mix to taste, then stir, lifting the flavours together. Garnish with the cherry tomatoes and lemon wedge skewered onto a cocktail stick, and the celery stick.

MAGNIFICENT MANGO SALSA

Serves 2

This fabulously colourful salsa recipe is bursting with fresh, fruity flavours – and also packs a wonderful Bajan warmth.

Fire Eater's Sauce Recommendation: Aunt May's Bajan Pepper Sauce (page 83)

Ingredients

1 large mango
½ red onion
2 spring onions (scallions)
1 red chilli (light–medium heat)
1 green jalapeño
Small bunch of fresh coriander (cilantro)
½ yellow bell pepper
½–1 tbsp Aunt May's Bajan Pepper Sauce (depending on how spicy you want to make it)
1 tbsp extra virgin olive oil
Salt and freshly ground black pepper

Method

Chop the mango, onion, spring onions (scallions), chillies, coriander (cilantro) and bell pepper and place in a large bowl. Add the sauce, olive oil and seasoning and mix thoroughly. Leave to marinate in the fridge for an hour for the best flavour. Serve with grilled chicken, fish, or our hot smoked beef ribs recipe on page 39.

SIZZLING CORNED BEEF HASH

Serves 2

Once considered a student store-cupboard staple, this underrated classic has had a bit of a renaissance lately – and it's easy to see why. A hearty, meaty and moreish delight, it is simple to make and a great base for experimenting with your favourite sauces.

Fire Eater's Sauce Recommendations: Don Gaucho (page 85) for a milder, more savoury heat; Crystal (page 48) or Frank's (page 53) for a drier, peppery burst of flavour

Ingredients

Small knob of butter
1 tbsp olive oil
½ red onion, diced
1 large white potato, peeled
    and diced
1 sweet ramiro pepper, diced
1 × 340g (12oz) can corned beef,
    diced into bite-sized pieces
    (chill it for easier chopping)
1 tbsp hot sauce
2 eggs
Small handful of fresh parsley,
    chopped
Salt and freshly ground
    black pepper

Method

Place a large wide pan over a medium heat, add the butter and oil and gently fry the onion and potato for about 5 minutes until slightly brown. Add the ramiro pepper and cook for a further 2 minutes, before adding the corned beef to warm through. Add some freshly ground pepper and the hot sauce and gently stir for a further 2–3 minutes.

In a separate pan, gently poach the eggs (try using white wine vinegar in the water to help keep the whites together), drain using a slotted spoon, and place on the hash. Sprinkle the parsley over the top, season and serve.

SMOKIN' TURKEY CHILLI

Serves 2

A lighter-style spicy one-pot dish. Perfect with rice, bread or tortilla chips.

Fire Eater's Sauce Recommendations: Condimaniac Smokey Dragon (page 112), Marie Sharp's Smoked Habanero (page 90), Valentina Salsa Muy Picante (see page 72)

Ingredients

2 medium onions, chopped
1 tbsp olive oil
4–5 garlic cloves, finely chopped or crushed
2 tsp cumin seeds
1 bell pepper (red, yellow or green)
1 chipotle pepper (the Mexican canned peppers in adobo are great and very convenient, or use dried and soaked chipotle, removing the seeds), chopped
500g (1lb 2oz) minced (ground) turkey breast
2 tsp smoked paprika
2 × 400g (14oz) cans good-quality chopped tomatoes
1 × 400g (14oz) can kidney beans
2 chunks good dark chocolate, at least 70% cocoa
½ tbsp Condimaniac Smokey Dragon (or to taste)
½ tbsp Marie Sharp's Smoked Habanero (or to taste)
½ tbsp Valentina Salsa Muy Picante (or to taste, optional)
Handful of fresh coriander (cilantro), chopped
Handful of grated (shredded) Cheddar or 1 tbsp sour cream
1 fresh lime
Salt and freshly ground black pepper

Method

In a large heavy pan gently fry the onions in oil over a low heat until they are soft and sweet, then add the garlic and cook gently for a few minutes.

Meanwhile, toast the cumin seeds in a dry pan for a few minutes, then grind using a pestle and mortar and add to the pan with the onions/garlic.

Char the bell pepper over a barbecue or under a grill (broiler). This adds a nice sweet smokiness. Remove the skin. Chop and add to the pan. Add the chipotle peppers, too.

Turn up the heat, add the turkey and stir fry until the turkey is evenly browned. Stir in the smoked paprika, then add the chopped tomatoes, kidney beans and the chocolate. Turn down the heat and cook gently without a lid for 20–30 minutes.

Taste to check for heat and seasoning. Add the Condimaniac Smokey Dragon for a lovely sweetness together with the Marie Sharp's for extra smokiness. If you want more heat, try adding some Valentina sauce, the black label version.

Remove from the heat and stir in the coriander (cilantro). Garnish with the Cheddar or sour cream and a squeeze of fresh lime.

WHIRLWIND VEGETABLE NOODLE STIR FRY

Serves 2

This hot and spicy Thai-influenced stir fry is a great vehicle for showing off a Sriracha in all its spicy, sticky goodness. The Shark brand is slightly thinner than some contemporary Srirachas and so makes for a terrific noodle sauce when combined with mirin rice wine.

Fire Eater's Sauce Recommendations: Shark Sriracha (page 152)

Ingredients

1 tbsp rice bran oil
1 medium pak choi (bok choy), roughly sliced
100g (3½oz) tenderstem broccoli
150g (5½oz) sugar snap peas, roughly chopped
1 mild red chilli, roughly chopped
1 bird's eye chilli, finely sliced (optional, dependent on your heat preference)
½ stick lemongrass, finely chopped
¼ red onion, sliced
250g (9oz) fresh bean sprouts
400g (14oz) fresh egg noodles
2 handfuls cashew nut pieces
½ handful fresh coriander (cilantro), finely chopped
1 spring onion (scallion), finely chopped (optional)

For the sauce
3 tbsp Sriracha (we use Shark)
2 tbsp mirin rice wine
¼ tsp of black pepper
¼ tsp salt
Squeeze of fresh lime

Method

Place a wok over a medium heat, add the rice bran oil and begin to gently fry the pak choi (bok choy), broccoli, sugar snap peas, chillies, lemongrass and red onion for 4–5 minutes. Add the bean sprouts, noodles and the sauce ingredients and toss to evenly coat everything. Cook for a further 2–3 minutes, before throwing in the cashew pieces. Remove from the heat and divide between two large bowls to serve. Sprinkle over the coriander (cilantro) and, if using, the spring onion (scallion).

For an additional kick, drizzle over some extra Sriracha, for example Huy Fong (page 58), Yellowbird (page 77) or Flying Goose (page 156).

VEGAN CHILLI-CHOCOLATE PEANUT BUTTER BROWNIES

Makes 8

An outrageously rich, moreish and moist brownie recipe that you can pimp to whatever level of heat you require.

Fire Eater's Sauce Recommendations: Singularity's Buy Ice Cream 'dessert' sauce (with moruga scorpion peppers, cocoa nibs and cherries – see page 142) or, for a milder, sweeter heat, Chorrito Hot Honey & Bourbon (page 114) – remember to halve the golden syrup if using a hot honey

Ingredients

2 small ripe bananas
125g (4½oz) smooth peanut butter
100ml (½ cup) golden syrup (corn syrup)
1½ tbsp coconut oil, melted
1 tsp vanilla essence
4 tbsp almond milk
25g (1oz) cocoa powder, finely sifted
1 tsp baking powder
¼ tsp salt
25g (1oz) ground almonds
1 small, mild red chilli, finely diced
Small handful of vegan dark chocolate chips
2 tsp hot sauce

Method

In a mixing bowl, finely mash the bananas and add the peanut butter, golden syrup, half the coconut oil, the vanilla essence and almond milk. Mix until smooth. Add the cocoa powder, baking powder, salt and ground almonds and fold into the mixture, until gooey. Stir in the diced chilli, chocolate chips and hot sauce, making sure to mix evenly.

Grease a small square brownie tin with the remaining oil (avoid anything too broad, or your brownies will be rather flat) and cook in the oven at 170°C/160°C fan (340°F/320°F fan) for 25–30 minutes until spongy on top but moist in the middle. Remove from the oven, allow to cool and then run a sharp knife round the edges. Gently slice into eight squares and cool further on a wire tray.

KICKIN' HOT SMOKED BEEF RIBS

Serves 2 (depending on how hungry you are)

This succulent, soft and deliciously sweet 'n' smoky rib recipe is absolutely perfect for a barbecue. Just give yourself enough time to prepare them – they're well worth the wait, we promise!

Fire Eater's Sauce Recommendation: Khoo's Heavy Smoker Chipotle sauce (page 127) or equivalent chipotle/barbecue sauce

Ingredients

4-bone rack of short ribs
4 tbsp chipotle or barbecue
   sauce

For the rub
1 tbsp sea salt
1 tbsp coarse black pepper
1 tbsp garlic powder
1 tbsp smoked paprika
1 tbsp onion powder

For the spritz
300ml (1¼ cups + 1 tbsp) apple
   cider vinegar

Method

Trim the excess fat from the top of the rack. Coat the ribs evenly in the chipotle sauce and leave to marinate for an hour.

Combine the rub ingredients and apply to the ribs evenly, ensuring all sides are covered.

In a smoker (or closed barbecue), hot smoke the ribs over apple or cherry wood for 3 hours at 130°C (265°F). Put the apple cider vinegar in a kitchen spray bottle and use it to spritz the meat once an hour. The cooling vinegar should help stop it from scorching and burning.

Remove the rack of ribs from the smoker and wrap in 3 layers of aluminium foil. Cook the wrapped ribs in the oven for 3 hours at 120°C (250°F). Unwrap the ribs and cook for a further hour at 120°C (250°F).

Remove the ribs from the oven. Separate the rack by slicing between the bones and serve on the bone.

PART 2

THE FIRE EATER'S HOT 101

Over the next section you'll find 101 of what we consider to be some of the most important hot sauces from around the world: a fine mixture of some absolute classics and plenty of new, original and downright brilliant beasts to tantalize the tongue. They come from a variety of locations spanning five continents, each one with its own soul and personality.

On page 170–171 we've brought them together in a quick-glance guide, ranked from mild to fire-eatingly brutal. Below is a key to our Fire Eater's Ratings, which will give you an idea of what to expect from each sauce:

MAGNIFICENTLY MILD

SUBTLE & WARMING

MODERATELY MOUTH-TINGLING

ALIVE & KICKING

STUPENDOUSLY SCORCHING

ULTIMATE FIRE EATER

NORTH AMERICA

ADOBOLOCO Hamajang

Adoboloco was founded – rather by accident, it seems – in Maui in 2010 after Hawaii-born-and-bred Tim Parsons and his wife Summer decided to plant some jalapeños for their young children in their home-school garden, which grew rapidly and successfully. Needing something to do with them, they established Adoboloco – the name comes from Tim's love of Filipino adobo, where chicken or pork is slowly marinated in vinegar, herbs and spices. After renting a community kitchen, the whole family – including children Scarlet, Harrison and Xander – pitched in to cook, bottle and label their wares. One of the family's bestsellers is their traditional Hawaiian Chili Pepper Water – a simple recipe that is popular across the islands.

Tasting Notes
Fine to medium in consistency. Fruity and tangy aroma with a smoky background. The flavour is very fruity with tart citrus notes from the peppers and vinegar. There is also a subtle smokiness that is perfectly balanced with the other flavours. The pepper burn builds slowly into an immense level of heat typical of the ghost pepper.

Origin Hawaii
(via Oregon), USA

Chilli Type smoked
ghost pepper

Fire Eater's Heat Rating

)))))

**Other Varieties
to Seek Out**
Taco! Tacoh!, a mixture of jalapeño, paprika and Trinidad scorpion, and Marionberry Splash!, made from a type of blackberry grown in Oregon, where Adoboloco also has a production kitchen.

Use It For
Great with wings or pork, substantial meat stews and soups. Lovely with Mexican dishes such as enchiladas and tacos.

adoboloco.com

BLAIR'S
Original Death Sauce

Origin Middletown, New Jersey, USA

Chilli Type red and orange habanero, cayenne and chipotle

Fire Eater's Heat Rating

Blair's Death Sauce was first conceived in 1989 by Blair Lazar, arguably one of the true pioneers of the Super Hot sauce movement, which has been tormenting the palates of millions of chilli-heads for decades. Lazar introduced his Original Death Sauce while he was still working as a bartender in New Jersey and it has gone on to spawn a range of other Super Hots, including an extremely limited-edition Reserve range, bottles of which have reportedly sold for thousands of dollars. Lazar has also released a limited-edition 16 Million Reserve, which has been certified by Guinness World Records as the hottest sauce of all time. Using pure crystallized capsaicin extract, it weighs in at 16 million Scoville units.

Tasting Notes
A fine to medium consistency, with an initial smokiness, and a meaty, complex flavour, with touches of coriander (cilantro) and lime. The heat arrives slowly – not a robust aggressive burn, but a pleasant warming, with lingering notes of lemon zest.

Other Varieties to Seek Out
Ultra Death, Mega Death, and Golden Death, a scotch bonnet-based recipe.

Use It For
Wings, a classic smoky sausage gumbo or jambalaya.

deathsauce.com

BÚFALO Salsa Picante Clásica

Búfalo sauce has a history that dates back over 90 years, to the company's humble beginnings in Monterrey in 1933. Today, it is widely regarded as one of Mexico's most popular sauces – and it's easy to see why. The recipe eschews the more sour/piquant styles of sauce made by the likes of Valentina and Cholula and uses dried guajillo peppers to bring a sweeter, smokier flavour. It's also considerably thicker and darker than most other sauces, giving it a deeper, richer, more meaty complexity.

Tasting Notes
Dark and thick, this has a very upfront spiciness: not unlike a traditional British brown sauce. Then comes an earthiness, with a dry, slightly smoky chilli note, with tamarind and deep dried fruit, such as figs or dates. The heat is mild, but well balanced enough to let you know it's there. A fabulously different addition to your sauce collection.

Origin Monterrey, Mexico

Chilli Type guajillo

Fire Eater's Heat Rating

Other Varieties to Seek Out
Búfalo Chipotle and Jalapeño.

Use It For
Any dark meat dish, or grilled sausages, which need some backbone but not too much heat that will mask the flavour.

salsas.com/bufalo

DAWSON'S Original Hot

What's the secret to a great hot sauce? A unique recipe? For sure. We'd also throw in a good measure of family support. Dawson's was founded in 2013 by Brodie Dawson and his father Bruce and the family bond has seen the business grow internationally. Brodie handles the creativity in the kitchen and Bruce the sales and promotional side of things. Fresh ingredients and the addition of extra-virgin olive oil helps the sauces really sing. Some interesting cultural nods include a Middle Eastern Shawarma Sauce in which cayenne pepper and honey are the lead flavours.

Tasting Notes
Thick and chunky in consistency, the initial flavour sings with fresh habanero. The sauce is also wonderfully sweet and unblended, giving a very textured experience. The heat is bold, but not overpowering and develops with a slightly tropical, honeyed note.

Origin Hamilton, Ontario, Canada

Chilli Type habanero

Fire Eater's Heat Rating

Other Varieties to Seek Out
The aforementioned Shawarma Sauce, Sichuan Ghost Pepper, and Big Smoke Chipotle.

Use It For
A great pizza sauce, and also, given the consistency, a superb base for spicy salad dressings.

dawsonshotsauce.com

CAJOHNS
Memento Mori

Origin Ohio, then North Carolina, USA

Chilli Type 7-pot douglah

Fire Eater's Heat Rating

CaJohns was founded in 2002 by 'The Godfather' of hot sauces, John 'CaJohn' Hard. His job as a fire-protection engineer took him to places such as Louisiana and Texas, where he acquired the taste for hot sauces. After many years of success, which saw the company's range expand to 150 different products, John decided to step back from the business, and CaJohns was bought out by its distributor, Hot Shots, in 2022.

Tasting Notes
Rich aroma of herbal tequila, some stewed apple, roast garlic and an almost chocolatey pepper note. The consistency is fine to medium with a few textured pieces. The taste is dry and spicy, with rich garlic balanced by fresh cider vinegar tartness. Then the heat hits: biting, angry and rasping. But it comes with a distinct nuttiness from the 7-pot douglah, leading to a warming, slightly tingling woody finish.

Other Varieties to Seek Out
La Segadora Reaper Hot Sauce, Black Garlic Hot Sauce, and Holy Jolokia Hot Sauce.

Use It For
Terrify your tacos with this: it's a brutal yet very honest sauce!

unitedsauces.com/collections/cajohns-fiery-foods

DIRTY DICK'S Hot Sauce

When someone has the sheer audacity to claim on the label that they make 'The World's Greatest Hot Sauce', you have to give it a try – if only to point out how they failed miserably. But in the case of Dirty Dick's, the hype could be entirely justified. The sauce was created by award-winning barbecue chef Richard Westhaver, who spent his childhood growing up in Montserrat in the Caribbean, learning to love the wares of the local chilli growers at the open-air market in Plymouth, the island's then main town. The theme is not blistering heat, but a focus on, as Richard explains, 'tropical fruits and sweetness'. Cue a series of almost yearly awards (now sitting at 75, including several at the prestigious NY Hot Sauce Expo) for his range. It makes you think Dirty Dick might be on to something.

Tasting Notes
Fine-medium consistency and a huge hit of tropical fruit freshness straight out of the bottle: mangos, ripe banana, dried fruits, including plump raisins and dates, some tamarind notes, and a layer of slightly drying Habanero beneath. The flavour is sweet and true to its tropical aromas, with an underlying heat that hits surprisingly quickly and lingers nicely, keeping the palate warm. Distinct, and definitely a sauce you need for your 'everyday dippers' collection.

Origin Vermont, USA

Chilli Type habanero

Fire Eater's Heat Rating

Other Varieties to Seek Out
Dick's Peachy Green, No Name Chipotle, and Dick's Caribbean Dream.

Use It For
Caribbean-influenced dishes, such as jerk chicken, or as a killer fruity/sweet salad dressing.

dirtydickshotsauce.com

HUICHOL SALSA Picante

Another Mexican classic, if perhaps not as widely appreciated as the likes of Valentina or Cholula, Huichol traces its origins back to 1949 and its founder Roberto López Flores, who at the time owned little other than a hand-mill and a few kilos of rattle chillies. He produced his sauce in small batches, sealing each bottle manually with crown caps. Today, the business produces 100,000 bottles a day, yet remains relatively humble, with a staff of just 20 people. Huichol is distinct because of its surprisingly intense upfront spiciness.

Tasting Notes
A medium-consistency sauce, with very direct notes of clove, cinnamon and black pepper right away. In fact, it's almost medicinal at first. Then comes the heat: a peppery dryness, with very little sweetness at all. The bite is restrained and balanced, but sits nicely on the palate, with the woody spice returning as an aftertaste.

Origin Jalisco, Mexico

Chilli Type cascabel chilli (also known as the little bell or rattle)

Fire Eater's Heat Rating

Other Varieties to Seek Out
Habanera, Limón (lime) and a spicier Negra (black) version.

Use It For
Steak, huevos rancheros (see page 30) and tacos.

salsahuichol.mx

CHOLULA
Original

Arguably the mother of all Mexican hot sauces, Cholula (pronounced Cho-loo-la) is based on a recipe developed by the Harrison family, originally from Chapala in Jalisco. The name originates from the Mexican town of Cholula, the oldest still-inhabited settlement in North America, dating back some 2,500 years. The brand is now owned by the Jose Cuervo company and this Original sauce is rated at 1,000–2,000 Scoville Heat Units.

Tasting Notes
Medium consistency, with a smooth texture. Initially salty, with a punch of vinegar, leading to an appealing aromatic dryness with paprika notes. Superbly complex and deep, with layers of warmth developing. Distinctively dry, with a hint of smokiness and a moderate rising heat.

Origin Mexico

Chilli Type chipotle, green pepper and sweet habanero.

Fire Eater's Heat Rating

Other Varieties to Seek Out
Búfalo Chipotle and Jalapeño.

Use It For
A Bloody Maria cocktail – with tequila instead of vodka (see page 33).

cholula.com

CRYSTAL
Hot Sauce

Origin New Orleans, USA

Chilli Type cayenne (used whole)

Fire Eater's Heat Rating

The sheer resilience of this brand is nothing short of amazing. Now celebrating its 100th anniversary, the Crystal story can be traced back to 1923 and the ingenuity of its creator, Alvin Baumer, who came to New Orleans after the Civil War. Baumer supposedly found the recipe inside an old abandoned drawer and his sauce became an instant hit with locals. In 2005 Crystal's 75-year-old production facility was destroyed by Hurricane Katrina. But you can't keep a good sauce down and it was soon replaced by a new facility outside the city, complete with a replica of its much-loved old sign. Today Crystal ships 450 million gallons worldwide, and the legacy of Alvin Baumer continues with third generation Alvin Jr at the helm.

Tasting Notes
Fine in consistency, Crystal is very fresh, vibrant and fruity in flavour, with a warming, toasted cayenne note, a well-balanced saltiness and a slow heat that creeps up on the palate.

Other Varieties to Seek Out
A garlic-heavy version, an Extra Hot and a Buffalo Sauce made especially for wings.

Use It For
A classic chicken gumbo, creole, sausage and shrimp jambalaya and Buffalo-style cauliflower bites.

crystalhotsauce.com

HELLFIRE Fear This!

Founded back in 2009 by Diana Papandrea, AKA 'The Sauceress' and Merle Mortensen, AKA 'The Chillimaster', Hellfire grew out of a love of fresh produce and Merle's 30-plus years experience of growing peppers. Their ingenuity has not only led to the creation of recipes using notoriously hot peppers such as the carolina reaper, bhut jolokia and Trinidad scorpion, but also ingredients as varied as mandarin oranges, chocolate, cinnamon, whisky and rum. Hellfire has won numerous awards and also partnered with renowned sculptor Dan Norton, who created a range of bottles that is now highly collectible.

Tasting Notes
Rich and thick in consistency, with a rugged, seedy texture. The aroma is complex and fruity, with dark sun-ripened tomato, smoky caramelized onion and a fresh, fruity pepper note from the reaper. The heat is explosive and upfront: bold, searing and quite dry with a long, lingering sting in the tail!

Origin Wisconsin, USA

Chilli Type carolina reaper

Fire Eater's Heat Rating

ۻۻۻۻۻ

Other Varieties to Seek Out
First Blood (a combo of bhut jolokia, red savina and other peppers), Fire Roasted Red Reaper & Garlic, and Kranked, Hellfire's award-winning black garlic and reaper combo.

Use It For
Fantastic as an accompaniment to rare char-grilled steak.

hellfirehotsauce.com

KANKUN Mexican Habanero Sauce

As a child, Rolando Cardenas sat around with his brothers watching his favourite lucha libre wrestlers valiantly battle each other on TV, the waft of his grandmother's home-cooked recipes in the air. Around that time he also became fascinated with Mexican cooking. Several decades later and the fully grown Rolando has proudly built a successful sauce business based on his family's traditional recipes and still finds the time to occasionally slip into a luchador costume to promote them.

Tasting Notes
Medium-thick in consistency, it has a simple flavour, with a vibrant habanero sweetness, mixed with a rising dry heat, a touch of saltiness and some tangy orange zest notes.

Origin Mexico

Chilli Type habanero and guajillo

Fire Eater's Heat Rating

ۻۻۻ

Other Varieties to Seek Out
Mexican Chipotle and a Mexican Jalapeño.

Use It For
Tacos and tortillas – both work well.

kankunsauce.com

DAVE'S GOURMET
Insanity Sauce

In the hot sauce world the name Dave Hirschkop is mentioned in hallowed terms. As the creator of a sauce widely agreed as the original 'hottest sauce on the planet', Hirschkop has almost certainly sealed his position in the canon of legends, but the story behind his original Insanity Sauce could have turned out very differently. As the owner of a Maryland eatery called Burrito Madness, he created the sauce as a way to deter unruly, drunken diners, but it had the opposite effect and people soon flocked to try his beastly elixir. Fast forward to 2022 and the Insanity Sauce has another 14 siblings, including a carolina reaper, a ghost pepper jolokia and the Ultimate Insanity Sauce!

Tasting Notes
Rich and thick in consistency, with a vibrant spicy aroma. The heat is almost instantaneous, with a dry lingering burn, some dried tomato notes and a zesty finish. Punchy and hot as hell, but with some deeper complexity too.

Origin San Rafael, California, USA

Chilli Type An undisclosed blend of peppers

Fire Eater's Heat Rating

)))))

Other Varieties to Seek Out
Cool Cayenne, Temporary Insanity, and the aforementioned Ultimate Insanity sauce.

Use It For
A few dashes in a chilli con carne with dark chocolate works really well.

davesgourmet.com

HOWLER MONKEY Original

Howler Monkey has endeavoured to produce an authentic Panamanian-style sauce (often called an Aji Chombo locally) and the recipe is about as natural as it gets: there are no thickening agents or preservatives to stop the sauce separating and it's all the better for it. The sauce also supports a number of causes looking after military veterans and service dogs.

Tasting Notes
A fine, silky consistency, with plenty of fleshy substance. After an initial blast of spicy, dry-heat pepper, the sauce becomes distinctly fruity, with some delicious notes of blood orange and sweeter bell pepper flavour. The overall heat is warming and well balanced.

Origin Jacksonville, Florida, USA

Chilli Type red scotch bonnet

Fire Eater's Heat Rating
)))

Other Varieties to Seek Out
Howler Monkey Verde, Amarillo (which uses yellow scotch bonnets), and a Hot variety, which combines scotch bonnets with red habanero peppers.

Use It For
Barbecue chicken skewers or glazed pork chops.

panamahotsauce.com

HEARTBREAKING DAWNS
1841 Ghost Pepper Hot Sauce

Founded in 2008 by two chefs, husband-and-wife team Johnny and Nicole McLaughlin, Heartbreaking Dawns began with the couple growing peppers in their garden in Arizona and turning them into homemade hot sauces. After producing a fairly 'regular' first three sauces, they soon began to experiment with more unusual ingredients, especially different kinds of fruit.

Tasting Notes
A fine consistency, with an upfront dark, fruity aroma and a tang from the ghost pepper, vinegar and lime. A brilliantly unusual mixture, based on pears and apple sauce. The flavour is initially fruity, with a warm caramel note, then becomes complex and rich, with hints of carrot and onion. A sharpness from the vinegar and lime balances the flavour. The jolokia heat builds slowly and is strong and long lasting.

Origin Arizona, USA

Chilli Type red habanero, bhut jolokia (ghost pepper)

Fire Eater's Heat Rating
))))

Other Varieties to Seek Out
1498 Trinidad Scorpion, 1542 Southwest Habanero, and Jalapeño Pineapple hot sauces.

Use It For
Fantastic with cheese, whether in a cheese omelette or on a pizza.

heartbreakingdawns.com

FRANK'S REDHOT
Original

Origin Buffalo, USA

Chilli Type cayenne, blended from both the USA and Mexico

Fire Eater's Heat Rating

An undisputed USA classic, Frank's can trace its ancestry back to 1918, when two partners, Adam Estilette and Jacob Frank, decided to explore blending varieties of cayenne pepper together. Jump to 1920 and Frank's was born. But it wasn't until 1964 that the Anchor Bar & Grill in Buffalo used Frank's as the base to create arguably the world's first Buffalo chicken wings. Today, Frank's is the number one selling American hot sauce, exported to over 20 countries.

Tasting Notes
Fine consistency and smooth in texture. Initial aromas are fresh limes, freshly cut red peppers, a slight coconut then smoked garlic note, with a hint of vinegar. The pepper is pronounced but not overpowering, with a mild bite, but gloriously fresh.

Other Varieties to Seek Out
Frank's RedHot Chile & Lime, Xtra Hot, and Sweet Chili.

Use It For
Has to be chicken wings, but also try a few dashes in a Margarita (see page 32).

franksredhot.com

HEARTBEAT HOT SAUCE CO
Scorpion Picante

Heartbeat Hot Sauce Co was founded in 2015 by Al Bourbouhakis and Nancy Shaw. The pair started out making hot sauce to enjoy for themselves as a hobby, but the company began in earnest after word-of-mouth spread through their hometown of Thunder Bay. All their sauces are made with home-fermented peppers, using traditional methods and are natural and free from preservatives.

Tasting Notes
A medium consistency. The aroma has notes of roasted red pepper, garlic and cumin. The initial flavours are the sweet and spicy pepper notes, with a touch of smoke, which balance beautifully with a sharp lemon and vinegar base. The heat kicks in a little later and is bold and long-lasting, with lingering fruity warmth and a slightly tart/dry note from the chillies.

Origin Ontario, Canada

Chilli Type habanero, Trinidad scorpion, and chipotle in adobo

Fire Eater's Heat Rating

))))

Other Varieties to Seek Out
Red Habanero, Blueberry Habanero, Jalapeño.

Use It For
This fresh and zingy sauce works well with the sweetness of fresh shrimp, or to brighten up a chicken or vegetable tagine. Very versatile.

heartbeathotsauce.com

HEATONIST
The Last Dab Apollo

Anyone with even a passing interest in hot sauce will be familiar with the internet phenomenon of Hot Ones, the hit YouTube show in which host Sean Evans torments celebrity guests with spicy chicken wings marinated in increasingly hotter sauces (seeing chef Gordon Ramsay almost in tears is priceless). The show culminates in a 'Last Dab' challenge that involves adding even more stupendously Super Hot sauce to the already searing wing. Of all the legendary sauces used for this segment, none has purportedly come as close to burning perfection as the Apollo, created by sauce company Heatonist in partnership with the legend that is Smokin' Ed Currie. Currie is famously the creator of the carolina reaper pepper (ranking between 1.5 and 2.2 million on the Scoville scale), pepper X (a drier-style Super Hot pepper), and now the apollo, a hybrid of the two that is supposedly even hotter. This is the only sauce in the world to feature the apollo and includes both fresh, dried and chilli distillate from the beastly pepper. You have been warned – or should that be 'warmed'?

Tasting Notes
Thick consistency, with a coarse texture. Absolute pandemonium on the palate. The heat is immediate and unrelenting, but alongside is a wonderful, fresh fruitiness. The flavour of the pepper is at the heart here, with only a touch of vinegar. As intense an experience as you will ever find… and totally worth it!

Origin Brooklyn, New York, USA

Chilli Type The Apollo

Fire Eater's Heat Rating

Other Varieties to Seek Out
The Classic Pepper X Edition, The Last Dab Reaper Edition, and The Last Dab XXX.

Use It For
You'd be crazy to try this on anything… but if you must, make it wings.

heatonist.com

HUY FONG
'Rooster' Sriracha

Origin Irwindale, California, USA (via Vietnam)

Chilli Type red jalapeño (formerly serrano)

Fire Eater's Heat Rating

Another enduring classic and a brand it's hard to imagine life without. It's also a company with an inspiring story behind it. Founder David Tran had begun making sauce in his home in Vietnam, but unrest in the late 1970s forced him to flee on a freighter ship named the *Huey Fong*, bound for Hong Kong. After he was granted asylum in the US in 1980, he set up Huy Fong, in homage to the ship that had ferried him to freedom. His brand of Sriracha was the first to make a real impression in the States, especially among the Vietnamese community, and today stands as one of the most important and influential condiments across the world. Huy Fong uses over 40,000 tonnes of fresh red jalapeños a year and its vast empire of spiciness sees no sign of being dented by the myriad copycat brands out there.

Tasting Notes
Medium consistency with a sticky texture. Unmistakable and distinctive, the aroma is a mixture of sweet and sour, with fresh peppers and vinegar leading the way, followed by a moderately pungent garlic. The flavour is surprisingly sweet, with a mouth-coating mixture of syrupy peppers, a punch of garlic and the sharpness of the vinegar. Balanced and distinctive.

Other Varieties to Seek Out
Chili Garlic and a Sambal Oelek fresh chilli paste.

Use It For
A classic with dim sum, or firecracker chicken noodle salad.

huyfong.com

KARMA SAUCE Cherry Bomb

Gene Olczak started his award-winning sauce company in 2010. A keen chef who enjoyed experimenting with the peppers and vegetables grown in his garden, he decided that hot sauce was his passion and resolved to make a product that was both healthy and sourced from local ingredients. As demand boomed, he and his family ended up buying a 23-acre farm in North Bristol, NY, to grow all the ingredients they needed. The Karma line now includes around 20 hot sauces, plus other condiments and spice blends. Incredibly, making hot sauces is not Gene's only job – by day he is an optical engineer who worked on Nasa's amazing James Webb Space Telescope!

Tasting Notes
Very rich on the nose, with the cinnamon and clove notes dominating along with a subtle coffee aroma, balanced by a sweet tang of sour cherry and apple cider vinegar. The taste is initially sweet and spicy, balanced with sharpness from the vinegar. The heat is hefty and long lasting with a slight, but not unpleasant, bitterness.

Origin Rochester, New York, USA

Chilli Type habanero

Fire Eater's Heat Rating

)))))

Other Varieties to Seek Out
Huhū Piña, Cosmic Dumpling, Scorpion Disco, Holé Molé.

Use It For
Great with chicken. The sweetness also pairs beautifully with duck.

karmasauce.com

LA MERIDANA Papaya Habanero

Founded in 2006, La Meridana is a family business that specializes in making sauces from locally grown Yucatán habanero peppers. The name is inspired by the women who in the past selected and harvested the chillies. Alongside the distinct properties of the habanero, this sauce also intertwines the sweet, tropical fruitiness of fresh papaya.

Tasting Notes
Fruit purée in consistency, with an initial light peppery heat, leading to a distinct, ripe fruitiness and fresh top note, alongside a subtle drying smokiness. The warming heat builds on the palate, but is never overpowering. Gentle, fruity, and all the better for it.

Origin Mérida, Yucatán, Mexico

Chilli Type habanero

Fire Eater's Heat Rating

Other Varieties to Seek Out
Mango Habanero, Green Habanero, Roasted Habanero, and Smoked Habanero.

Use It For
Fruit-based salsas, hard cheeses such as Parmesan, and tuna ceviche.

lameridana.com

LA PREFERIDA Louisiana-Style Hot Sauce

La Preferida's story starts in the 1920s when German immigrant Henry Steinbarth established a meat market on the south-west side of Chicago and, recognizing the opportunity to serve the needs of the many Mexican families living and working in the area, began to sell chorizo sausages. The business flourished and became known as 'La Preferida' – 'the preferred choice' – and a brand was born. From 1949, La Preferida began developing more Mexican and other regional culinary products, including salsas and sauces, such as its hugely popular Louisiana-style pepper sauce. Today the company is still in family ownership and its heritage as a true American classic is sealed.

Tasting Notes
Fine in consistency, with a smooth texture. All the hallmarks of a Louisiana sauce are here: a piquant, dry, savoury aroma of cayenne peppers, sharp vinegar and a nice balance of saltiness and pepper on the palate. The heat is relatively mild in contrast to the fresh savoury flavour, but the formula remains a winning combination.

Origin Chicago, USA

Chilli Type cayenne

Fire Eater's Heat Rating

Other Varieties to Seek Out
N/A

Use It For
Fried eggs, and classics such as corned beef hash (see page 35).

lapreferida.com

PUCKERBUTT PEPPER COMPANY
The Reaper

Pioneering, brilliant and a little bit bonkers – that is probably a fair assessment of Smokin' Ed Currie, founder and main man behind PuckerButt Pepper Company sauces. As the creator of the notorious carolina reaper, certified as the world's hottest chilli pepper in 2017 by Guinness World Records (which rated it at 1,641,183 SHU), Smokin' Ed understands better than anyone else how to integrate heat into a sauce. His The Reaper set a new standard for just how dizzyingly brutal-yet-tasty Super Hot sauces can be.

Tasting Notes
Medium consistency with a wonderful seed-heavy texture. The initial aroma and flavour is super-fresh and fruity, with raspberry and blood orange notes. Then comes the heat: a swirling hurricane, rather than a knock-out blow to the face. It's intense, slow burning and beautifully balanced, never overstepping the fruitiness of the pepper itself. In a world where Super Hot can mean one-sided, this is still dynamic and enjoyable.

Origin South Carolina, USA

Chilli Type carolina reaper

Fire Eater's Heat Rating

Other Varieties to Seek Out
Smokin' Racha (a riff on a habanero-based Sriracha), Gator Sauce (using Currie's pepper X variety of pepper), and Reaper Squeezins (made from 92% pure natural carolina reaper).

Use It For
With this level of heat, use it sparingly in a citrus marinade, or throw caution to the wind and slather it over hot chicken wings.

puckerbuttpeppercompany.com

TAPATÍO Salsa Picante

Tapatío is another true American success story in the world of hot sauce. The brand was founded in 1971 by Jose-Luis Saavedra, Sr as a modest operation in Maywood, California and has continued to grow ever since, with the company celebrating its 50th anniversary in 2021. Salsa Picante is the only sauce in the Tapatío stable, but it does boast maybe the largest – and wackiest – set of merchandise of any hot sauce company!

Tasting Notes
Medium consistency, with a classic dry chilli flavour and a solid balance of saltiness and vinegar piquancy. The heat is restrained but mouth-coating and warming. Salsa Picante has a long, peppery aftertaste.

Origin California, USA

Chilli Type unknown

Fire Eater's Heat Rating

Other Varieties to Seek Out
A limited edition collaboration with Gabriel Iglesias, AKA 'Fluffy'.

Use It For
Huevos rancheros (see page 30), seared tuna steaks and grilled chicken skewers.

tapatiohotsauce.com

MEET THE SAUCERER:
Erica Diehl, Queen Majesty Sauce, New York, USA

If any sauce deserves to receive a royal seal of approval, it's Queen Majesty. Founder Erica Diehl tells us about her Jamaican influence and love of unusual combinations.

Tell us about your route into the world of hot sauce...

The shorter version of the story is that I grew up in Buffalo, NY, and I believe that everyone in Buffalo has a bottle of Frank's hot sauce in their fridge! I've always loved that vinegar bite and pepper warmth. I really loved making my own hot sauce and so, in 2013, I decided to start selling my favourite creation, the Scotch Bonnet & Ginger Hot Sauce. The name Queen Majesty is actually from a song named 'Queen Majesty' by The Techniques, a Jamaican group from the 1960s. I chose that name not only because it was feminine and confident, but also because I had been using it as a DJ name for over 10 years at the time. I only play Jamaican music and that was a big Jamaican hit song.

What's the secret behind a great hot sauce?

Beautiful ingredients and balance.

What or who has been your biggest influence in creating the successful recipes you have worked on?

My biggest influence would be the friends I did yearly [sauce-making] competitions with. We were all just winging it and being creative and learning as we went. This was over 15 years ago, so the information online was not like it is today. I remember looking at Tabasco hot sauce ingredients – peppers, vinegar and salt – and using that as the base and experimenting from that starting point.

Have you come across any surprising pairings of hot sauces and foods/drinks?

I don't have a sweet tooth at all, but I tried some pancakes with spicy syrup and fruit and it is SO good! I sprinkled our Ancho Habanero Hot Sauce Powder over them but I think it could also work with cayenne or straight ancho powder. These peppers are from Mexico and, of course, in Mexican cuisine they incorporate chillies in such beautifully brilliant ways, such as in chocolate and with fruit. I really want to bake a very spicy chocolate cake!

Can you pick a hot sauce made by someone else that you can't live without?

I'm a huge fan of Marie Sharp's Habanero Pepper Sauce. Really nice.

What are the essentials in the hot sauce-tasters' tool box – i.e. what are the best antidotes for calming a searing palate?

Patience, time and a steel stomach – ha! I don't like milk so I can't recommend that, but they say it helps. I usually just ride the wave.

Finally, try to sum up Queen Majesty in just three words...

Warmth, balance, joy.

QUEEN MAJESTY
Scotch Bonnet & Ginger Hot Sauce

Erica Diehl is the 'saucerer' behind Queen Majesty. At various times she has worked as a graphic designer and a reggae DJ (which she still does under the name Queen Majesty). She began making sauces for herself in the early 2000s after growing frustrated with the limited range available in shops at the time. Around 2013, business started to flourish. All the Queen Majesty range is handmade in NYC, using only natural and fresh ingredients, organic where possible, with a strong ecological and social conscience.

Tasting Notes
The aroma on opening the bottle is full of wonderful lemon and ginger notes, combined with distinctive scotch bonnet pepper fruitiness. Some toasted coconut scents begin to develop after a while. The taste is light, slightly sweet and super zingy, with a strong warmth from the peppers and ginger. All in all, a perfectly balanced sauce.

Origin Queens, New York, USA

Chilli Type scotch bonnet, habanero

Fire Eater's Heat Rating

Other Varieties to Seek Out
Jalapeño, Tequila & Lime, and Red Habanero & Black Coffee.

Use It For
Fantastic with an oily fish like salmon or a chicken taco. Also amazing in a whiskey hot toddy if you are feeling a little under the weather and need warming up.

queenmajestyhotsauce.com

SECRET AARDVARK
Habenero

All great businesses start with a truly clear visionary – and in Scott Moritz, the vision to become a culinary creator started early, at the age of 13 in a local chilli cook-off. After developing a pie business, a tamale cart and a thriving restaurant called Salvador Molly's, he started Secret Aardvark sauces in 2004, working hard to gain a foothold in the various Portland food markets. Tragically, Scott passed away in 2009, but his legacy has been valiantly carried on by his former partner, Stacy, and Secret Aardvark has grown into one of the most exciting and vibrant sauce brands in the USA. Sustainability and community run deep in the DNA of the company – a percentage of the profits go to support local music charities (Scott was an avid local musician) and the distinctive Aardvark-clad plastic bottles are made locally, to reduce the firm's carbon footprint.

Tasting Notes
Very thick in consistency, with immediate spice and a fresh herbaceous and carrot flavour, alongside a sun-dried tomato note and citrus bite. The heat is subtle, but develops into a warming sweet, mouth-coating experience.

Origin Portland, USA

Chilli Type red habanero

Fire Eater's Heat Rating

Other Varieties to Seek Out
A Serrabanero green sauce (a blend of serrano and habanero chillies) and a Smoky Aardvark Chipotle.

Use It For
Makes a great Red Eye cocktail (beer, tomato juice, hot sauce, salt and a squeeze of fresh lemon juice) and an awesome, no-nonsense hot dog topping.

secretaardvark.com

TABASCO
Original

Origin Avery Island, Louisiana, USA

Chilli Type red tabasco

Fire Eater's Heat Rating

It's hard to imagine a world without this ubiquitous red-topped bottle. In fact, there's no doubt that without the labours of founder Edmund McIlhenny, the culture of hot sauce and culinary habits in the USA, UK and Europe would be distinctly different – and all the blander! McIlhenny created his famous brand after growing his first commercial crop of peppers in 1868 and perfecting the process of maturing the mash (chilli, vinegar and salt) in American white oak casks (the same ones used for maturing American whiskey). Today the company remains under family ownership, with sixth-generation Harold 'Took' Osborn still personally inspecting each batch of the mature mash. The recipe and process remain largely the same, with the mash ageing for three years to develop its distinct piquancy.

Tasting Notes
Fine consistency and smooth textured. Distinct and iconic: the chilli brings a fresh zestiness, alongside a sweeter, fruity note. The balance of salt and vinegar is perfect, with a drier, peppery aftertaste and a warming heat.

Other Varieties to Seek Out
Habanero, Raspberry Chipotle, Green Jalapeño, and Scorpion varieties, alongside a newly released Sriracha sauce.

Use It For
Just about everything: from a Bloody Mary (or Maria – see page 33) to fresh oysters.

tabasco.com

SMALL AXE PEPPERS
Ghost Pepper Hot Sauce

Origin New York, USA

Chilli Type bhut jolokia (ghost pepper) and habanero

Fire Eater's Heat Rating

Small Axe is the brainchild of NY-based chef King Phojanakong (a pioneer in the burgeoning US Filipino food movement), Dan Fitzgerald and John Crotty. Crotty is an affordable housing development officer in the Bronx who established the company back in 2015, purchasing peppers grown in local community gardens and urban green spaces. In the process Small Axe has helped turn underused and undervalued areas into vibrant, pepper-growing paradises for the local community and has since expanded to the national level. It now works with an incredible 120 community gardens in 42 cities (from Baltimore to Oakland, California) in 24 states across the USA. The net result is that every bottle of sauce sold benefits and directly supports the gardeners and local growers. A great cause, with great flavour to boot!

Tasting Notes
Thick consistency with a wonderfully rugged texture. The aroma and flavour showcases a deep, complex and slightly smoky pepper note, with a habanero freshness and then layers of sweet tamarind, dates and caramelized onion. The heat is restrained but creeping, slowly emerging on the palate to give a lingering warmth.

Other Varieties to Seek Out
The Chicago Red Hot Jalapeño, The Bronx Greenmarket and The Atlanta Georgia Peach.

Use It For
Gives a wicked kick to scrambled eggs and smoked salmon. Beware: a little goes a long way!

smallaxepeppers.com

MEET THE SAUCERER:
Harold 'Took' Osborn, Tabasco, Louisiana, USA

The most iconic hot sauce brand in history also comes with over 150 years of family heritage. Took Osborn shares his experiences of maintaining that legacy.

Tell us about your route into the world of hot sauce. Being part of such an incredible family business must have been an amazing journey...

It certainly is an incredible legacy to be a part of. For six generations, dating back to 1868, my family has owned and operated the McIlhenny Company. Ever since I was a kid this company has been a huge part of my life. In fact, my first job with the company was as a stock boy in the employee deli at the age of eight years old. Since joining the company in an official capacity, I've held positions in different departments; most recently as head of international marketing before taking on my current position as CEO. Travelling the world gave me lots of insight into the ways people from different cultures use hot sauce to add excitement to their food. It's been such a rewarding journey!

What would you say is the secret behind a truly great hot sauce?

For Tabasco, it's all about the recipe, the process by which it is made and the ingredients – red peppers, salt and distilled vinegar – it remains virtually unchanged. Consistency in the process and an unwavering commitment to quality, by my family and the generations of families who have worked alongside us, are vital to our success.

The barrel-ageing process is a huge part of Tabasco. What does this bring to the recipe that can't be replicated elsewhere?

Every bottle of Tabasco Original Red sauce starts with our pepper mash. The mash is aged for up to three years in white oak barrels that are tightly sealed with a layer of thick salt on top. Over the course of this three-year ageing process, it evolves and matures, which then gives the sauce its signature flavour. Every barrel is stored in our mash warehouse on Avery Island for consistency in the process.

Any tips you can give people looking to work on their own first hot sauce recipe?

I think believing in yourself and your product is the most important thing. Edmund McIlhenny certainly didn't set out to create the global company we run today, but without his dedication and hard work back in 1868, Tabasco wouldn't exist as we know it.

Are there any surprising pairings of foods/drinks with your hot sauces that you have unexpectedly come across?

Well, of course, I believe that our sauces work well with all foods. Whether you're eating something sweet, savoury or a drink. I have been experimenting with putting both our green and red sauces in salad dressing recently. I've always viewed greens as something you HAVE to eat, but I have to admit, I really like the kick our sauce adds to a dressing and the way it makes salads more interesting. I'm also obsessed with making my own pasta. Half a teaspoon of red sauce added to the eggs as you're making the dough really lights it up.

Finally, try to sum up Tabasco in just three words...

Three simple ingredients.

VALENTINA
Salsa Picante

Origin Guadalajara, Mexico

Chilli Type Mexican-grown puya chilli

Fire Eater's Heat Rating

One of the most enduring of all Mexican hot sauces, Valentina was first introduced back in 1954 and is produced by the Salsa Tamazula company, which also has a line of hot sauces under that name. Valentina takes its name from Valentina Ramírez Avitia, a legendary Mexican revolutionary, who gained notoriety as one of the few women to enlist and fight against the Federales during the Mexican Revolution in the early 1900s. This original 'Red Label' version (actually yellow in colour!) is distinctly pourable and designed to serve as everything from an accompaniment to meats to the base in a marinade.

Tasting Notes
Fine to medium consistency and smooth texture. Distinctly peppery, meaty and savoury, with an additional vibrant citrus note and a touch of maltiness. The heat is mild and warming, rather than hot.

Other Varieties to Seek Out
A superb, hotter 'Black Label' and a 'Blue Label' Marisquera version specifically designed for seafood.

Use It For
Delicious drizzled on beef or pork tacos.

salsavalentina.com

TEXAS PETE
Original

Back in 1929, founder Sam Garner and his son Thad purchased a restaurant in their home town of Winston-Salem, which also included the secret recipe for a barbecue sauce. The restaurant failed, but the sauce – made in their home kitchen – thrived and the father and son duo later joined with two of Sam's other sons to form the TW Garner Food Co, with numerous sauces and products to its name. Legend has it that this now classic name may never have existed if the Garners had taken the advice of a marketeer, who suggested an alternative. Luckily Sam intervened and he was proven right. Texas Pete: a legend was soon born!

Tasting Notes
A very fine consistency, with a dry, and distinctly savoury note upfront. The sauce has a mild heat with a little prickle on the tongue, alongside a little zesty lime note emerging.

Origin Winston-Salem, North Carolina, USA

Chilli Type cayenne

Fire Eater's Heat Rating

Other Varieties to Seek Out
Texas Pete Hotter, ¡Sabor! Mexican-Style sauce, and Cha! Sriracha sauce.

Use It For
Lighter, sweeter shellfish, such as crab, crayfish and lobster.

texaspete.com

TORCHBEARER
Son of Zombie

You know the saying, two's company, three's a crowd? Well that definitely doesn't apply to Vid, Ben and Tim, the chaps behind Torchbearer sauces. The three friends came together over a surplus of habaneros that had been growing in their gardens and decided to make some preserve. Turns out it was pretty good and they wanted to take things further. So, after a frankly insane 72-hour drive from Pennsylvania to Texas and back, they emerged with 666 pounds of additional habaneros and began crafting a sauce long into the night. The result ended up winning a bunch of awards at the Cajun Hot Sauce Festival in Louisiana and the rest is history. This sauce is a mixture of a trio of their other recipes: Chipotle Barbeque, Honey Garlic and their fan-favourite Zombie Apocalypse. Three definitely seems to be the magic number for these boys.

Tasting Notes
Medium consistency and a hugely complex blast of aromas from the get-go – a slight smokiness, plump tomatoes, rich brown sugar and a sweet citrus lead into a nicely drying aroma of pepper. The taste is huge: more of the sweetness and smokiness, but with a delicious, gently rising heat, some ripe, fleshy pepper notes and caramelized onion. A really well-balanced and truly delicious sauce.

Origin Pennsylvania, USA

Chilli Type ghost pepper and habanero

Fire Eater's Heat Rating

Other Varieties to Seek Out
The Rapture (a Trinidad scorpion-based sauce), Plum Reaper, Honey Badger, and Sweet Onion Habanero.

Use It For
Lovely as a wing sauce, over blue cheese on a burger, or on grilled chicken skewers.

torchbearersauces.co

YELLOWBIRD
Blue Agave Sriracha

Austin has always been a city synonymous with creativity (every year it plays host to the South by Southwest music and film festival), so it's no surprise to find a sauce company as creative as Yellowbird taking up residence there. Founded by Erin Link and George Milton in 2013, Yellowbird brings together unusual pairings (blue agave nectar in its Sriracha), as well as organic creations using locally grown fruit and vegetables.

Tasting Notes
A rich consistency, the sweetness leaps off the tongue, with a honeyed fruitiness. Big, ripe tomato notes mix with a fruity, zest-laden tingle, while an upfront spicy heat subsides slowly into a lovely mellow finish.

Origin Austin, Texas, USA

Chilli Type red jalapeño

Fire Eater's Heat Rating

)))

Other Varieties to Seek Out
Organic Ghost Pepper, classic Jalapeño, and a green Serrano sauce.

Use It For
A spicy chicken black bean salad.

yellowbirdfoods.com

EL YUCATECO
Salsa Picante Roja de Chile Habanero

El Yucateco was started in 1968 by Priamo José Gamboa Ojeda in Yucatán, Mexico. Gamboa made and sold his homemade habanero hot sauces and condiments locally, and today El Yucateco is one of the bestselling habanero hot sauces in the US, offering five different varieties, plus jalapeño and chipotle versions and a host of other condiments.

Tasting Notes
A distinctive aroma of tomatoes, peppers and spices on opening the bottle. An initial taste of sweet tomatoes, laced with complex spices and a lovely fruity habanero kick. The pepper heat builds to a significant warmth that is long lasting.

Origin Yucatán, Mexico

Chilli Type habanero

Fire Eater's Heat Rating
))))

Other Varieties to Seek Out
El Yucateco Chile Jalapeño sauce and Salsa Picante Verde de Chile Habanero.

Use It For
Great with prawns (shrimp) and works perfectly in a Bloody Mary.

elyucateco.com

CARIBBEAN & SOUTH AMERICA

AMAZON PEPPER CO Green Amazon

Amazon Pepper Co was founded in 1994 in Valle del Cacua, Colombia, and exclusively uses peppers grown around the Amazon Basin. These include the namesake Amazon, which has a unique flavour and freshness that the company only discovered by accident after it rescued a batch due to be thrown away (the light green, yellow-tinged peppers looked nothing like the ones it had been using up to that point). Other pepper varieties in its sauces include cayenne, jalapeño, scotch bonnet, habanero and bhut jolokia, which Amazon's parent company has been cultivating since 1974. The two flagship sauces, Green Amazon and Red Amazon, both use high concentrations of peppers in their recipes.

Tasting Notes
Thick in consistency, with a fleshy texture. Very fresh and herbaceous aromas hit first, with just a touch of vinegar and seasoning. The flavour is green and vegetal, with a nice latent, bright heat that arrives slowly.

Origin Colombia

Chilli Type amazon

Fire Eater's Heat Rating

)))

Other Varieties to Seek Out
Red Amazon, Guava, Mango, Chipotle, Ghost Pepper, and Habanero sauces.

Use It For
Superb drizzled over white fish tacos.

amazonpepper.com

ENCONA West Indian Original Hot Pepper Sauce

Origin Jamaica (via the UK)

Chilli Type habanero and scotch bonnet

Fire Eater's Heat Rating

Part of the Grace Foods empire, which can trace its Jamaican heritage back to 1922, Encona arrived as the Windrush Generation began searching for authentic Caribbean flavours and products in the UK. In 1975 it introduced its West Indian Original Hot Pepper Sauce, which has remained a Caribbean staple in British kitchens ever since. Today Encona is Britain's number one selling hot sauce brand and has developed a wide range of international flavours, from Jamaican Style Jerk BBQ to Indian Mango Chilli, and Louisiana Cajun sauces.

Tasting Notes
Really fresh and vibrant, with a medium, seed-heavy consistency. The heat is restrained, allowing the other fruit-laden flavours to evolve first. Fresh tomatoes, some sweet demerara (light brown) sugar and very fresh, ripe red scotch bonnets develop, with a hint of tamarind, some ripe banana and a well-balanced vinegar note.

Other Varieties to Seek Out
South Carolina Reaper Sauce, Jamaican Scotch Bonnet Sauce, and West Indian Exxxtra Hot Pepper Sauce.

Use It For
Jerk pulled pork with fried rice, or mix a little with hot butter to pour over popcorn.

enconasauces.co.uk

AUNT MAY'S
Bajan Pepper Sauce

An absolute Caribbean classic and no mistake. Aunt May's was first created over 30 years ago in the small town of St Michael's Parish in Barbados and retains its unmistakable Bajan charm to this day. Using scotch bonnets alongside a healthy amount of mustard, it is a distinct, wholesome and inviting experience.

Tasting Notes
Medium consistency with plenty of chopped pepper. The initial flavour is a creamy mustard note, leading into an underlying heat-laden palate of the scotch bonnets, which bring a fresh fruitiness and a lingering zesty kick. It's bold, but not outrageous, with a more delicate complex side too.

Origin Barbados

Chilli Type scotch bonnet

Fire Eater's Heat Rating

))))

Other Varieties to Seek Out
Aunt May's Red Pepper Sauce.

Use It For
A mango or pineapple salsa (see page 34 for a suggested recipe).

aunt-mays.com

BARON West Indian Hot Sauce

Baron is a St Lucian stalwart in the hot sauce world. Established in 1991 with a handful of employees, the company has been manufacturing a range of classic sauces for over 30 years, from the original West Indian, which combines hot pepper and mustard and has won numerous awards for its flavour and heat, through to a Blazing Hot Sauce that uses ground scotch bonnet peppers. Baron produces sauces in St Lucia, Grenada and Trinidad.

Tasting Notes
Extremely thick in consistency, it has an immediate blast of dry heat, with a combination of slightly herbal flavour and a fruitiness from the peppers (of which we suspect a proportion are scotch bonnet). The liveliness continues on the palate, with a more creamy fruitiness developing that leads to a slow, warming and dry finish.

Origin St Lucia

Chilli Type undisclosed

Fire Eater's Heat Rating

$$\rangle\rangle\rangle\rangle$$

Other Varieties to Seek Out
Classic Pepper Sauce and Blazing Hot Sauce.

Use It For
Honey-and-oil salad dressings and tropical fruit salsas. It's also good used as a marinade.

baronfoodsltd.com

CHIEF Scorpion Pepper Sauce

Chief dates back to 1957 and is one of the most successful food companies in the Caribbean. But the road to success was far from easy for founder Sayeed Khan. The grandson of Ahamad Khan, an Indian labourer who suffered the hardship of the plantation indentureship system, Sayeed worked at his father's grocery shop before becoming a fireman for the local military base aged just 17. He went on to found a small rice-milling business, which then began to produce packet curries and coffee, before developing into other condiments such as hot sauces. Today, the company exports to over a dozen countries and sells a range of six hot sauces.

Tasting Notes
With a fine-to-medium consistency, the sauce has a huge initial fruitiness on the nose, with fresh, tropical notes, and a distinct fragrant pepper. The flavour is equally tropical with some sweet, charred mango and papaya. Then comes the heat: a huge wave of powerful scorpion sting hits – and lingers. It's dry and unforgiving, but equally tingling and exciting. An unexpected delight and hot as hell.

Origin Trinidad and Tobago

Chilli Type Trinidad scorpion

Fire Eater's Heat Rating

Other Varieties to Seek Out
Lime Flavoured, a classic Chunky Red, and a Yellow variety.

Use It For
The heat means the sauce is ideal for seasoning rich, meaty dishes, such as mutton stew or goat curry.

chief-brand.com

DON GAUCHO Chimichurri Picante

Chimichurri is important in Argentinian cuisine. In fact, it is so entwined with the culture of steak there that preparing one without the other is almost inconceivable! Don Gaucho has been producing a variety of Chimichurri sauces for over a decade and their authenticity of flavour has brought them to the attention of renowned Buenos Aires-born chef Chakall, who uses them across his restaurant empire in Portugal.

Tasting Notes
Wonderfully meaty and rich, with a thick, course consistency. The heat is surprisingly punchy upfront, with a dry, slightly smoky/roasted chilli note developing first. The balance is fatty and mouth-coating with plenty of deep, resonant chilli flavour, black pepper and wine vinegar.

Origin Argentina

Chilli Type cayenne pepper

Fire Eater's Heat Rating

Other Varieties to Seek Out
Salsa Gaucha and Chimichurri Original.

Use It For
It has to be a perfectly cooked char-grilled steak – either a sirloin or an ojo de bife (ribeye).

don-gaucho.com

D'VANYA'S Junkanoo Hot Pepper Sauce

Over the past 20 years, D'Vanya's has become a national treasure in the Bahamas and endeared itself to the palates of thousands of visitors with its range of traditional spicy sauces and condiments. The secret? The goat pepper, a descendant of the *Capsicum chinense* family of peppers and a relative of the scotch bonnet that resembles a tiny yellow/orange pumpkin. The goat has a similar heat to a habanero, but its burn is perhaps less dominant. D'Vanya's has aimed to capture the spirit, colour and playfulness of the Bahamian Junkanoo carnival in this sauce and, for the uninitiated, it certainly tastes like a whole lot of fun!

Tasting Notes
Fine-to-medium consistency. The aroma is full on fruitiness and fresh pepper, with a touch of something tropical. There's some fried onion/tomato scent and flavour, a jab of citrus and a very bold, sweet/spicy mouth-coating texture. The heat rises surprisingly swiftly, just to the point of raising a smile, then subsides into a pleasant warmth.

Origin Nassau, Bahamas

Chilli Type goat pepper

Fire Eater's Heat Rating

Other Varieties to Seek Out
D'Vanya's Original Bahamian Hot Pepper, Tamarind Hot, Mango Pepper and Guava Pepper sauces.

Use It For
Jerk chicken, seafood stew and grilled white fish.

dvanyas.com

LÉGAL HOT SAUCE
Medium

A Brazilian hot sauce using the unique power of the Malagueta, a long, fine pepper said to have been discovered by Portuguese explorers on their travels in South America. It is supposedly a lucky plant, given that it was often found growing near where hauls of gold were discovered. The Légal range offers three heat levels and the recipe uses carrot to give additional body.

Tasting Notes
Medium consistency, the heat is nicely rounded and balanced – this 'Medium Heat' variety packs enough of a punch to feel distinct without overpowering. The flavour is sweet, with an emerging dryness and slight smokiness, and a clean, dry pepperiness from the chillies.

Origin Brazil

Chilli Type malagueta pepper

Fire Eater's Heat Rating

Other Varieties to Seek Out
Légal Mild and Hot versions.

Use It For
Lobster rolls, deep-fried squid rings and other shellfish dishes.

legalhotsauce.com

LOTTIE'S Original Barbados Recipe Hot Pepper Sauce

For a sauce considered a national treasure and so widely available internationally, Lottie's is surrounded in mystery! Information about its production, history and recipe is very limited, save for a few cryptic facts – such as the lady behind the brand is not a fan of hot foods herself! Suffice to say that alongside Aunt May's (page 83) and Windmill Products' sauces (page 100), this is an absolute essential in your collection of Caribbean sauces.

Tasting Notes
Fresh and buttery on the nose, the sauce has a fine-to-medium consistency with plenty of seeds and flesh. The flavour is bold and ripe: big, fresh habanero peppers hit first with a deep, rich fruity tomato-like note, before a citrus buzz of fresh orange juice and touch of dried fruit follow. Refreshing and mouthwatering.

Origin Barbados

Chilli Type habanero

Fire Eater's Heat Rating

Other Varieties to Seek Out
Lottie's Traditional Barbados Recipe Yellow Hot Pepper Sauce.

Use It For
A great accompaniment to a Bloody Mary or, if you enjoy gin, a Red Snapper.

No website, but widely available

MARATÁ Gota Picante Molho de Pimenta Verde

Founded by José Augusto Vieira in the 1960s, Maratá is one of Brazil's most successful companies, originally producing tobacco products, roasting coffee and supplying tea. It also produces a range of well-known pepper sauces, which have become popular on restaurant tables and in domestic kitchens across Brazil.

Tasting Notes
Fine in consistency and instantly fresh and citrussy. The green pepper note is direct and upfront (think crunchy green jalapeño), with an abundance of freshly squeezed lime juice flavour and a pleasant white wine vinegar tartness. It has a simple, but refreshing balance.

Origin Brazil

Chilli Type unknown

Fire Eater's Heat Rating

Other Varieties to Seek Out
Gota Picante Molho de Pimenta, a red pepper version.

Use It For
Lovely on scrambled eggs on toast or with a Portuguese-style sausage and egg tortilla.

marata.com.br

MATOUK'S Trinidad Hot Sauce

A firm favourite across the Caribbean, Matouk's hot sauce is a Trinidad speciality and very much treated as a condiment, like mustard or ketchup – which is apt, given the size and shape of the bottle. It has a light to medium heat and combines the dual punch of mustard and scotch bonnet.

Tasting Notes
Very thick and creamy in consistency, with plenty of seeds and shredded chilli pieces. The sauce is thick on the palate too, with a pickled note (the scotch bonnets are pickled, rather than fresh or dried), which gives it a much more savoury-led flavour. The heat is restrained, with a little prickle of warmth that really hits the sides of the tongue. All in all, this has a lot in common with spicy piccalilli.

Origin Trinidad and Tobago

Chilli Type scotch bonnet

Fire Eater's Heat Rating

Other Varieties to Seek Out
Trinidad Scorpion, Calypso, and Soca (which uses hotter, aged pickled peppers).

Use It For
Cold meats and cheeses. It also makes a great hot sandwich spread.

facebook.com/matouks

WALKERSWOOD Scotch Bonnet Pepper Sauce

Hailing from the hills of St Ann in Jamaica, Walkerswood was established in 1978 with the firm aim of developing local community prospects in its rural location. It was the first company to export jerk seasoning from Jamaica, and Walkerswood works closely with a cooperative of local farmers to grow the scotch bonnet peppers it uses to produce its sauces. It also has a pepper seeding nursery programme that gives plants back to the community to continue the steady flow of local produce.

Tasting Notes
Medium consistency with a chunky, seed-heavy composition. The sauce is very dry and savoury at first, with a latent heat that slowly builds up. A bold punch develops, with a pleasant creamy aftertaste packed with sweet onion notes.

Origin Jamaica

Chilli Type yellow scotch bonnet

Fire Eater's Heat Rating

Other Varieties to Seek Out
A 'Seriously Hot' Jonkanoo sauce.

Use It For
Salted cod fish and ackee.

walkerswood.com

MARIE SHARP'S
Habanero Pepper Sauce

Marie Sharp's is one of the world's leading brands of hot pepper sauce and a true hot sauce institution. Marie began selling sauces locally from her kitchen in her native Belize in 1981. As their popularity grew, so did Marie's reputation and she built a full-scale production facility in 1985 to cope with demand. Today, Marie Sharp's employs over 100 people, 85% of whom are women, while the great lady herself is rightly hailed as the 'Queen of the Habanero'. Legendary status without doubt.

Tasting Notes
On opening the bottle, the aroma is noticeably vegetal, the earthy carrot combining with the fruitier habanero. The first taste is fresh and lively lime, combined with a slight pepper dryness. Then you're hit by the delicious flavour of sweet carrot gently sautéed in butter. The heat is prominent throughout and continues to build after the buttery flavours have dissipated. The consistency is fine, with small textured bits of the fresh ingredients.

Origin Belize

Chilli Type red habanero

Fire Eater's Heat Rating

))))

Other Varieties to Seek Out
Green Habanero Pepper Sauce (made with nopal cactus), Pure Love Pineapple Habanero Sauce, and Beware Comatose Heat Level Habanero Pepper Sauce.

Use It For
Very versatile, it makes a delicious addition to scrambled eggs and is fantastic with fried chicken.

mariesharpsusa.com

MEET THE SAUCERER:
Jody Williams, Marie Sharp's, Belize

Belize-based Jody Williams has lived and breathed hot sauce his whole life, thanks to his grandmother's extraordinary contributions to the cause.

So, tell us about your route into the world of hot sauce... Was it love at first bite, or did something else make you fall head over heels for them?

I was born into it! Mrs Marie Sharp, my grandmother, founder and creator of Marie Sharp's Hot Sauces, had begun making a unique hot sauce in her kitchen in 1981, combining it with fresh vegetables or fruits grown right here on our family farm. She worked out of her kitchen for many years until she got her first factory in the late '80s. By that time, I was already a three- or four-year-old, running through the factory watching my grandma and other family, like my dad, working together to create one of the best sauces Belize has to offer to the world. However, it wasn't until 1996 (I will never forget this...) that I took my first taste of my family's hot pepper sauce. It was a very hot Saturday day at the Belize Chamber of Commerce Expo and on top of that I was very hungry. I went ahead and dipped a soda biscuit into the Green Nopal Pepper Sauce. My taste buds lit up and then I dipped another soda biscuit, followed by another, then another. I soon paid the price, though, because I was running around the show ground looking for milk or water to calm the heat in my mouth. Since that day I was hooked for life!

What's the secret behind a great hot sauce?

A great sauce is one that we can use daily on our favourite food and we would feel incomplete if we didn't use it. A great sauce is also one that we praise and share with our family and friends for its taste, quality and origins. Moreover, a great sauce must have the finest clean ingredients. In addition, behind a great hot sauce is its leader and team who work endlessly on a daily basis to make a consistent, high-quality product that everyone can enjoy.

Is the chilli pepper's flavour as important as the heat in the hot sauces you make?

Marie Sharp's main focus is flavour over heat. It's also about having the right balance. In our sauces you can taste the vegetables or fruits along with the kick of spice that you feel at the same time. Each sauce is unique. We have over 16 different flavours of sauces ranging from mild, to a very spicy Red Hornet Lava Heat sauce. I always say eating hot sauce is like training or running a marathon. You start slowly and gradually increase the distance over time.

Any tips you can give to readers working on their first hot sauce recipe?

Choose quality over everything, especially at the start, and let it be consistent for the long haul. Once quality is established and maintained, consumers will be back for more in no time. Also don't use shortcuts in your process. Today hot sauce lovers and consumers want more than a spicy hot sauce – they also want clean ingredients and a nice story behind it. Always have a mindset to improve and innovate. The beauty with hot sauces is that we can make them from any type of food base – papaya, celery, spinach, even coffee! With this mindset we can adapt to the fast-changing and booming global hot sauce markets.

Have you come across any surprising pairings of foods/drinks with hot sauces that just work brilliantly together?

In Belize we love our Marie'Ladas, which is a Michelada [a beer, mixed with lime juice and hot sauce] made with Marie Sharp's hot sauces. We also love our hot sauces with ketchup on our garnaches and tacos here. Some people mix our Sweet Pepper Sauce with vanilla ice cream, which is super delicious! I've come across bars mixing spirits with hot sauces and the result is a powerful drink with a kick of spice. Also the younger generation mix our hot sauces on their oranges and other fruits – fiery orange or pineapple anyone?

Do you have a favourite food/drink recipe that uses your hot sauce?

Our national dish is rice and beans, which cannot go without my favourite hot sauce, Marie Sharp's Fiery Hot. Also I love to add the Belizean Heat Habanero Pepper Sauce to my BBQ sauce before adding it to chicken or other meat.

What are the essentials in the hot sauce taster's tool box: i.e. what are the best antidotes you've come across to help calm a searing palate?

A jug of milk, yogurt and some cream cheese! When the burns get going, only those three can help bring down the heat.

What's next for you – any new sauces on the way?

We are looking into using more exotic fruits to add more hot sauces to our portfolio; for example a dragonfruit-habanero fusion and also some spice-specific sauces, such as a Spicy Ginger Caribbean Sauce. Since we will be doubling production capacity, we will have more time to create more great sauces for you all.

Finally, try to sum up Marie Sharp's in just three words...

Fresh, Love, Belizean!

PICKAPEPPA
Hot Mango Sauce

Pickapeppa is an unquestionable legend in the world of Jamaican cuisine. Created in 1921, the original recipe is so popular that it has become known as 'Jamaican Ketchup', gracing the tables of thousands of homes for decades. Now its popularity has also begun to spread worldwide, and its unique blend of spices and peppers is ideal for everything from jerk chicken to burger sauce. One of its signature serves is even to pour it over a block of cream cheese! The range has developed to five standout sauces, including a limited edition Hot Pepper variety that is rarely produced and sells out almost immediately. Supermodel Naomi Campbell is said to take a bottle of Pickapeppa with her wherever she travels. If it's good enough for Naomi, it's good enough for us. A classic.

Tasting Notes
Fine-to-medium in consistency and smooth in texture. The initial aromas and flavours are very fruity indeed, with a big whack of fresh mango, some spicy dried fruit and well-cooked onion, all sitting nicely with a wash of punchy vinegar. The heat is warming and tingling – not brutal at all – and develops with a slow intensity, balancing with the sweetness of the mango as the flavours develop.

Origin Jamaica

Chilli Type unknown

Fire Eater's Heat Rating

Other Varieties to Seek Out
The original (a store-cupboard essential), Hot Pepper, and Gingery Mango.

Use It For
You have to try the cream cheese serve. As crazy as it sounds, it's delicious with freshly toasted bread.

pickapeppa.com

RICANTE Fire Melons

The Ricante story is an envious tale: Royce Mitchell found himself needing to escape the rat race and in 2008 decided Costa Rica might be just what he was looking for. In 2011 he began to dabble with his first sauce, Mango Caliente, when the island had a surplus of fruit. The rest is history. Ricante (a portmanteau of *rico*, meaning 'delicious' in Spanish, and *picante*, meaning 'spicy hot') now offers a multitude of incredible, fresh-tasting sauces – including Fire Melons, a mouthwatering mix of cantaloupe melon, kiwi and habanero – available in over 1,000 locations in the US.

Tasting Notes
Medium consistency, with a lovely smooth texture. The aromas are refreshing sweet melon, a pulsating green kiwi note, and the radiance of fresh habaneros. Equally refreshing on the palate at first, it quickly becomes pretty blistering, with a spiky blast of pepper that leads into a lingering, tingly fruit flavour and peppery warmth.

Origin Costa Rica

Chilli Type habanero

Fire Eater's Heat Rating

)))))

Other Varieties to Seek Out
Mango Caliente, Piña Dulce (with mango and pineapple), and Manzana Encendida with habaneros, apples, mangos and carrots.

Use It For
Chicken skewers. It also makes a great way to scorch up a fruit salad.

ricante.com

MENDEZ HOT SAUCE

With a strong community-minded spirit, Mendez produces a unique style of hot sauce, built around a Brazilian farming collective. Seventeen years ago, Rafael Mendes was visiting central Brazil and discovered the flavour of the malagueta pepper (see page 86). Deciding to make a vegan-friendly sauce, he set about creating Mendez, which has a distinct creamy style, not dissimilar to a hot mayo. Given its need for native malagueta peppers, the brand now works closely with a number of specific farming families, guaranteeing a fair price for their crop. Mendez prides itself on the fact that every 5,000 bottles of Mendez Hot Sauce sold supports a Brazilian farming family for one year.

Tasting Notes
Citrus note and vinegar tang, the heat level is mild, but distinct enough to deliver the requisite punch when paired with a variety of dishes.

Origin Brazil

Chilli Type malagueta pepper

Fire Eater's Heat Rating

**Other Varieties
to Seek Out**
N/A

Use It For
Churrasco (skirt) steak
with home-cooked fries.

mendezhotsauce.com

WINDMILL PRODUCTS
Hot Pepper Sauce

Windmill has passed its heritage down through four generations of the Millers, the family who originally founded the company. Made to the same recipe for over 100 years, it's another undisputed Bajan classic and one of the most popular sauces in Barbados.

Tasting Notes
A sweet mustard aroma with a tang from the peppers. The soft and buttery mustard taste is surprisingly creamy, while the heat from the chillies is prominent in the aftertaste but delivers warmth rather than harshness. The texture is creamy smooth and dotted with little chunks of onion and pepper.

Origin Barbados

Chilli Type scotch bonnet

Fire Eater's Heat Rating

)))

Other Varieties to Seek Out
Hot Bajan Ketchup.

Use It For
Supremely versatile – try it with ham, as a sandwich spread, on hot dogs and burgers, and add to gravies and stews for a mustard-pepper kick.

No website, but find them on Facebook

PRODUCT OF BARBADOS

hot
pepper sauce
SHAKE WELL

WINDMILL PRODUCTS

INGREDIENTS: WATER, RIPE
PEPPERS (15%), ONIONS,
MUSTARD FLOUR, SALT, STARCH,
SUGAR, ACETIC ACID,
PRESERVATIVE - E202.

AFRICA

BLACK MAMBA Cayenne Chilli Sauce

A love affair with the raw ingredients and a friendly competitive streak are sometimes all it takes to create an empire... and for Joe Roques and Claudia Castellanos, this is how the incredible success of Black Mamba came to fruition. Joe, a native of Eswatini, started to explore making his own hot sauce in his kitchen back in 2010, ominously calling it Black Mamba. With a little creative remixing from Colombia-born Claudia, they produced their first batch of 400 bottles, which sold out at a local music and arts festival. Today, Black Mamba has grown into a business that ships across four continents and supports a strong female workforce. It has also partnered with Guba, a local permaculture NGO representing 50 smallholding farms, to provide its fresh herbs and peppers, supporting some 1,000 Eswatini locals in the process.

Tasting Notes
Medium to thick consistency and a slightly chunky texture, with pepper and seeds. Wonderfully fruity and herbaceous on the nose, with a slightly smoky cayenne note. The sauce explodes with flavour, including pungent ginger, a little vinegar bite, some zingy citrus and lots of warming pepper notes.

Origin Eswatini

Chilli Type cayenne

Fire Eater's Heat Rating

Other Varieties to Seek Out
XXXtra Hot Peri-Peri (with carolina reaper), Pineapple Chilli Sauce, and Habanero and Jalapeño sauces.

Use It For
Drizzled on a rare steak, or with a homemade kebab.

blackmambachilli.com

JOHNNY HEXBURG
Chocolate Bhutlah

Origin South Africa

Chilli Type chocolate bhutlah

Fire Eater's Heat Rating

Sometimes the inspiration for a name can strike in the oddest of places. For Marihett and Derek Bredenkamp, it came from their three-year-old son. Founded in 2016, Johnny Hexburg is the name of their little boy's super-cool imaginary friend. Hexburg is the buddy we all wish we had, the hero fighting by our side in imaginary battles, and the rock star accompanying us on stage, and he provides the perfect identity for the couple's fabulous hot sauce recipes, which have not only taken South Africa but the whole global sauce community by storm. Marihett and Derek still craft all the sauces themselves using South African-grown chillies, including reapers, 7-pots and, in this one, the rather unusual chocolate bhutlah.

Tasting Notes
Fine-medium in consistency with a slight fleshy texture. The aromas explode with dry, peppery exotic spice, with cinnamon, anise, cumin, cloves and turmeric. It's dark, complex and brooding. Then the heat arrives as an arid whirlwind on the palate. It's biting and unforgiving, but never oversteps the spice and complexity, with a prickly dryness that lingers and numbs the lips.

Other Varieties to Seek Out
Gunslinger (Hexburg's hottest sauce), 7 Pot Barrackpore, Hot Paper Lantern and a CBD-infused sauce.

Use It For
A medium-rare t-bone steak, as part of a butter sauce. The dryness really brings out the sweetness of the meat.

johnnyhexburghotsauce.co.za

NALI Hot

Origin Malawi

Chilli Type bird's-eye

Fire Eater's Heat Rating

Nali has reached something like cult status in its native Malawi – and it's easy to see why. The brand was conceived in 1974, when Nali-Lo Khoromana discovered bird's eye peppers growing on the shore of Lake Malawi. Over four decades later, his family have continued producing the sauce to his distinct recipe.

Tasting Notes
Thick in consistency with a seed-heavy texture, the initial aromas are of dry chilli and vinegar piquancy. The sharpness gives way to a light citrus note and a warmer, spicy chilli aroma. The flavour is initially hot and punchy, with a dry, almost toasted chilli flavour, coupled with a hint of paprika-led smoky sweetness.

Other Varieties to Seek Out
Nali Kambuzi, Garlic, and Gold.

Use It For
Works well as a marinade with olive oil for char-grilled white fish, such as cod or hake.

naligroup.mw

CHIKA CHIKA Fire Roasted Tamarind Chilli

Beginning in 2014, the Chika Chika story is one born out of necessity. Although Zaheed and Arzoo Dewji had access to local markets abundant with fantastic spices and peppers, they were disappointed about the lack of quality Kenyan-made hot sauces – and so decided to do something about it. After working on some family recipes, they hit on a range of super fire-roasted pepper ideas, bringing in a wealth of other locally grown ingredients, including tamarind, mint and coriander (cilantro).

Tasting Notes
Medium consistency with a smooth texture. The first flavours are a combination of distinct, sweet tamarind, dark brown sugar and tangy vinegar. The heat arrives swiftly: initially dry and very direct, it leads into an almost medicinal pepperiness and a pleasant warming bite, with lingering notes of soft fruit.

Origin Mombasa, Kenya

Chilli Type pili pili

Fire Eater's Heat Rating

)))

**Other Varieties
to Seek Out**
Chika Chika X-tra Hot, Mango Chilli, and Mint Chilli, using green demon peppers.

Use It For
Really good with barbecue sausages and lamb chops.

planetchika.com

DR TROUBLE
Double Oak Smoked Chilli

Dr Trouble is created and bottled on founder Rob Fletcher's farm in the upper Zambezi valley. As Rob explains: 'My great-grandfather created the original recipe 130 years ago and when I found it scrawled in the back of a book two decades ago, I knew this could be something special!' The brand has a philanthropic side and a proportion of each bottle of Dr Trouble sold benefits the Little Peppers Project, which is run by Rob and provides school fees and essential supplies for 150 local village children. Dr Trouble is 100% organic and, unusually, also lemon based, meaning no vinegar is used. It is fermented in custom-blown glass flagons out in the Zambezi sun for 100 days.

Tasting Notes
On the nose there is the pungency of fenugreek, a rich smokiness and a slight citrus tang. The first flavour to arrive is a big whack of lemon, but it is smooth and not eye-watering. Then the spices come through, enveloped in a wonderful smoky haze. The heat is mild to warming but very balanced, with a prominent smoky aftertaste.

Origin Zimbabwe

Chilli Type red bird's eye and cayenne

Fire Eater's Heat Rating

Other Varieties to Seek Out
Dr Trouble Lemon Chilli.

Use It For
Versatile with its low heat, it is great with barbecue meats and cold-cut sandwiches.

drtroublesauce.co.uk

MEET THE SAUCERER:
Rob Fletcher, Dr Trouble, Zimbabwe

The founder of Dr Trouble has long championed the unique aspects of African hot sauce – and the world is really taking notice!

Tell us about your route into the world of hot sauce. Was it love at first bite, or did something else make you fall head over heels for it? Also, where did the name Dr Trouble come from?

I guess my love for spice came from my father. I have been using the famous Piri Piri on my food since I was a teenager. I was born in Africa – fourth generation. Africans love some spice in their food. You can find chilli sauce along all the highways, where a common snack is freshly roasted maize cobs – each vendor will have salt and a bottle of very hot chilli sauce to add to it. The name Dr Trouble came from a nickname I had in my twenties – my friends started to call me 'Trouble' and one day someone said, 'He's not just trouble, he's the doctor of trouble.'

What's the secret behind a great hot sauce?

I believe the secret of a great hot sauce is to not overpower the palate. A hot sauce should accentuate the eating experience without destroying the flavour of the food being eaten. Too many hot sauce products focus on trying to be the hottest, at the expense of flavour.

What, or who, has been your biggest influence in creating the successful recipes you have worked on?

Our recipe is 130 years old, and came from the diaries of my great-grandfather. He was a surveyor and drew the first maps of the country. My father and I found a simple recipe among his archive of papers, and we decided to make some, using chillies from our vegetable garden. Each year we tinkered and experimented with different chillies and spices. We ended up doing this every year for 15 years until he passed away. So I guess my greatest influence would be my ancestors.

Any tips you can give anyone working on their first hot sauce recipe?

Don't be afraid to experiment! I see so many people following the same time-worn path to making hot sauce. One of the reasons for our flavour success is the fact we are one of the only products not using vinegar. We use only fresh, squeezed lemon juice: a blend of wild-grown lemons (harvested around the foothills of the Zambezi valley) with eureka lemons to boost the tartness. Don't be afraid to break some rules – there's magic to be found.

Have you come across any surprising pairings of foods/drinks with hot sauces?

I've always loved the South American street snack of fresh sliced mango and chilli. The sweetness of cold mango with the bite of heat creates a wonderfully unlikely alliance.

Can you pick a hot sauce made by someone else that you cannot live without?

Without doubt, I cannot live without Mr Vikki's East India Chilli Pickle. A masterful concoction!

Finally, try to sum up Dr Trouble in just three words...

Always all natural.

LE PHARE DU CAP BON
Harissa

Not strictly a 'hot sauce', but when talking about the culture of chilli sauce it is impossible not to include Harissa, the key accompaniment to tagine and other mouthwatering north African dishes. Le Phare du Cap Bon is arguably the most famous, if not the original, brand of this fiery red paste. Its iconic yellow packaging and lighthouse logo date back to 1946 and symbolize the Cap Bon Peninsula in north-eastern Tunisia. Still produced to the same recipe of different peppers, garlic, coriander, caraway seeds and sea salt, this is an undisputed classic.

Tasting Notes
Thick in consistency with a smooth, paste-like texture. The smell from opening a fresh can is worth the price alone: vibrant smoky pepper, bold spice, with distinct caraway notes. The flavour is initially slightly sweet, leading into a punchy, upfront dry heat with a salty, smoky undertone. Truly wonderful and unique. An absolute must-have for the kitchen and any hot sauce collection.

Origin Tunisia

Chilli Type unknown

Fire Eater's Heat Rating

Other Varieties to Seek Out
N/A

Use It For
A classic lamb shank tagine (served with a healthy dollop on the side to mix in) or stirred into the sauce of a rustic tomato and meatball dish.

scapcb.com

EUROPE

CONDIMANIAC Smokey Dragon

Condimaniac was started in 2018 by London-based couple Jen Dreier and Kier Kemp. They started as fans, reviewing hundreds of hot sauces on their Instagram account @Condimaniac, before deciding it was time to put their knowledge to use making their first sauce, Smokey Dragon.

Tasting Notes
A lovely smoky tomato aroma with a tang of onion. First taste is a rich sweetness from the vine tomatoes, which is balanced by the sharpness of apple cider vinegar and lime juice. The medium heat is quite intense, perhaps from the komodo dragon pepper, and it lingers long with a subtle smokiness.

Origin Kent, England

Chilli Type serrano, komodo dragon, chipotle

Fire Eater's Heat Rating

Other Varieties to Seek Out
Kyubi Hot Sauce, Séance Hot Sauce.

Use It For
Add some big splashes to your chilli con carne for a rich sweet heat. Also fantastic on chicken or beef tacos.

condimaniac.com

CHILLI OF THE VALLEY
Pasilla Queen of the Dessert

Origin Merthyr Tydfil, Wales

Chilli Type pasilla

Fire Eater's Heat Rating

Chilli of the Valley was founded in 2012 by father-and-son team Arwel and Dan Reed. Inspired by Arwel's legendary curries, Dan was an early convert to the hot side. They now grow all their own chillies in the beautiful Welsh Valleys and their ingredients are sourced as locally as possible.

Tasting Notes
The aroma is packed full of beautiful raspberries, with a slight note of lime, while the consistency is smooth to medium. This is an unusual hot sauce, a one-of-a-kind in this book, as it is specifically made for desserts. It tastes like a rich, sweet raspberry compote freshened up by a subtle lime sharpness. The pasilla chilli, in powdered form, adds an earthy, chocolatey note to the ensemble. The heat is mild and works well in the context of a dessert-led sauce.

Other Varieties to Seek Out
Superior Peri, Sir Cha Cha, Samurai Mango.

Use It For
Ice cream, sorbet, apple pie.

chilliotv.co.uk

CHORRITO SAUCE CO
Hot Honey & Bourbon

With over 20 years in the food and hospitality industry, Chorrito Sauce founder Dan Bentlett knows exactly how to combine a few quality ingredients to create a range of condiments that can elevate everyday food. Dan's passion for food started at a young age and was ignited through his love of travel. His trips took him from Syria to South America, sharing meals and stories with local families, discovering different cuisines and an abundance of spice. Then, in 2018, what started as an experiment using local organic chillies soon became a business as he began selling his small-batch hot sauce recipes.

Tasting Notes
The smell is of good honey with a slight fruitiness from the reaper peppers. The consistency is fine – lighter than a typical runny honey – and the flavour is predominantly of quality honey, sweet without being cloying. The reaper pepper brings a rich fruitiness and the bourbon adds a lovely depth to the flavours. The tingling reaper heat arrives at a medium level and lingers long in the mouth.

Origin Edinburgh, Scotland

Chilli Type carolina reaper

Fire Eater's Heat Rating
)))

Other Varieties to Seek Out
Jalapeño/Apple/Tequila, Habanero/Orange/Coffee, and Reaper/Cafe Patrón/Charcoal.

Use It For
Great with desserts, ice cream, chocolate mousse, awesome on a pizza, and makes a killer extra-hot toddy.

chorritosauce.com

CRAZY BASTARD
Ghost Pepper & Mango

Bonkers, brilliant and completely irreverent – three words that perfectly sum up Berlin's Crazy Bastard. A love of the absurd and a fear of – well, very little – led company founder Jonathan O'Reilly to create his first sauce in his home kitchen in 2013. His passion for haloing the pepper type as the absolute star and only using oven-roasted chillies, fresh fruit, tomatillos, and fine Italian vinegar with no added sugar has since spawned seven killer recipes to punish the palates of dedicated devotees. As well as opening a restaurant (Crazy Bastard Kitchen), CB has done a few collaborations, including a recurring one with uber-cool DJ and producer Nightmares on Wax. In 2021 it celebrated making its 400,000th bottle of sauce. Keep on being Crazy Bs, chaps!

Tasting Notes
Thick in consistency and very fleshy in texture. The aromas of ripe mango hit home first, with subtle spice (some cumin notes) and a lovely creaminess on the palate. Then the heat smashes in: wave one is purest ghost – prickly and peppery, with a real deep burn – then wave two delivers a drying sucker-punch with a real tongue-coating warmth and sharp lime juice note. It lingers and nips at you all the way down, all the time reminding you of how fruity it is too.

Origin Berlin, Germany

Chilli Type ghost pepper (bhut jolokia)

Fire Eater's Heat Rating

Other Varieties to Seek Out
A Super Hot pack of Scorpion, Naga, and Reaper pepper sauces; Habanero & Tomatillo and Jalapeño & Date.

Use It For
Try this as a popadom or naan dip if your curry needs pepping up.

crazybsauce.com

DEVIL DOG SAUCES
Jalapeño & Pineapple

A small-batch company based in Manchester making an exciting and unusual range of sauces. Owner Liam Kirwan used to be a professional chef and ran a pop-up restaurant, which ignited his love of spices. His experiments with other commercial sauces led him to work on his own, focusing predominantly on the flavour of the peppers, rather than the heat. A decade later, his award-winning range of sauces is now stocked in many locations around the globe and spans over a dozen recipes.

Tasting Notes
The first thing to hit is a caramel sweetness from the demerara (light brown) sugar, and then a lovely, deep pineapple flavour bursts through alongside more subtle coconut and carrot notes. The heat builds slowly and is warm and mild, but never harsh. All delivered with a silky-smooth texture.

Origin Manchester, England

Chilli Type habanero

Fire Eater's Heat Rating

**Other Varieties
to Seek Out**
Carolina Reaper, Blackberry & Lemon Thyme; Scotch Bonnet, Mango & Lime; Naga Viper, East Asian Spiced Plum & Raspberry.

Use It For
Amazing with a grilled cheese sandwich or to spice up vanilla ice cream.

devildogsauces.co.uk

MEET THE SAUCERER:
Liam Kirwan, Devil Dog Sauces, Manchester, England

The main man behind Manchester's Devil Dog Sauces spills the beans on his love of fresh peppers and his passion for creating new recipes.

Tell us about your route into the world of hot sauce...

My introduction to sauce began about nine years ago. I was hosting a pop-up in London and one of the dishes on the menu needed a hot sauce. This started my journey down the rabbit hole. While researching existing brands and trialling recipes, my tolerance grew and grew. The pop-up eventually ended but my love of chilli was just beginning.

What would you say is the secret behind a truly great hot sauce?

This is easy. FLAVOUR! FLAVOUR! FLAVOUR! Most, when asked what's the first thing they think of when they hear the word chilli, would say heat, but this is a disservice to an amazing fruit. Chillies are a magical ingredient. Whether it's the earthy smoky warmth of a chipotle or the fiery citrus fruits of a scotch bonnet, they give so much to whatever they are added to.

Why do you think people are so obsessed with the pain/pleasure aspect of hot sauces?

Why do people jump out of planes? We are all attracted to risk and danger at some level. With chillies the pain represents the danger; taking an unnecessary risk in turn gives us the serotonin boost as a reward. Also capsaicin gets the blood flowing and the heart pumping a little faster, making us feel a little more alive!

Have you come across any surprising hot sauce/food and drink pairings?

At a hot sauce festival last year, customers were drinking margaritas and one lady put our Jalapeño and Pineapple sauce into hers. It was amazing. Also hot sauce and ice cream together. The hotter the sauce, the crazier the sensation in your mouth of pain and instantaneous relief. It's a real trip!

Is there a hot sauce made by someone else that you can't live without?

Wow, this is tough. I can't say there is one I can't live without, but the sauce used the most in our house that is not one of ours is Yoyo Laos Sauce (see page 158). It is so tasty. Honourable mentions go to Slim Jim's Sriracha and Double D's Pineapple Tabasco.

Any new recipes on the horizon?

There are always new sauces en route. I've been getting back into my raw ferments recently, which opens another run in the rabbit hole of hot sauce. We have a Green Cayenne Chimichurri in the works, along with a naga viper, raw cocoa and burnt orange ferment. If I could, I would have a new flavour for every day. The long-term goal is to create a hot sauce using only ingredients native to these shores. Watch this space.

Finally, try to sum up Devil Dog in just three words...

Flavour. Fire. Passion.

CROOKED PICKLE CO Nero Black Pepper Hot Sauce

Crooked Pickle Co was founded in 2018 by Felix Mendelssohn after he spotted a gap in the market for gourmet pickled veg more inventive and interesting than standard supermarket fare. The company has also developed a small range of interesting hot sauces, including Nero, one of the only hot sauces we could find that uses no chilli peppers at all. Instead it delivers its heat purely by black pepper. The name Crooked Pickle was inspired by the famous twisted spire of Chesterfield's Church of St Mary and All Saints.

Tasting Notes
The initial aroma is the distinct tingle of freshly ground black pepper, but there are also darker notes of the black garlic and coconut charcoal. The consistency is medium-thick. Bright, fruity and vinegary on the tongue with an intense ground pepper flavour. It also has an unusual resinous darkness: perhaps it's the pepper or the activated charcoal. Not unpleasant, just very unusual! The burn is there, different from a chilli heat, but there's an overall warmth that's medium in strength and one that lingers long with the peppery flavour.

Origin Chesterfield, England

Chilli Type No chilli! Just black pepper

Fire Eater's Heat Rating

Other Varieties to Seek Out
Bango Nero, Pinero.

Use It For
Try with simple plain pasta and grated (shredded) Parmesan cheese. It will also give your mashed potatoes a punch and can work with stronger mature cheeses.

crookedpickle.co

FIRELLI Italian Hot Sauce

A very different take on traditional hot sauce, Firelli, hailing from Parma, has gone to great lengths to bring a distinctly national feel to the recipe: roasted red peppers, balsamic vinegar and porcini mushrooms all give an unmistakable italiano flavour. The sauce was designed primarily as an accompaniment to pizza, but the Italian soul that runs so deeply through it makes for a very accessible and fun sauce indeed. *Buon appetito!*

Tasting Notes
Medium consistency and smooth. The first aromas are of charred pepper, a slightly umami savoury note and some rich wine vinegar. The flavours are equally distinct: the porcini mushroom is particularly noticeable, alongside a dark, fleshy pepperiness. The heat is mild and restrained, with a little prickle developing as the sauce settles on the tongue.

Origin Parma, Italy

Chilli Type unknown

Fire Eater's Heat Rating

Other Varieties to Seek Out
An Extra Hot, with added cayenne pepper, and a Truffle Hot Sauce, with umami notes.

Use It For
A classic margherita pizza, but also drizzled into penne arrabiata.

firellihotsauce.com

GABKO
Hot Pepper Sauce Red

Origin Hungary

Chilli Type carolina reaper, scorpion and naga jolokia

Fire Eater's Heat Rating

'And the 2020 Scovie Award goes to... Hungary!' You can imagine the joy in New Mexico when Gábor Nagy learned his sauce had won arguably the most prestigious prize in the business. But the founder of Gabko was already used to winning, having scooped a heap of top awards for his sauces since 2016. It's a remarkable achievement for a man who began growing peppers and making sauces as a hobby in 2011. Gábor's two main sauces, titled Red and Yellow, are simple to describe, with a high pepper content (as much as 80%), but big, bold and beautiful – flowing with fresh pepper taste, and packing plenty of blistering heat to boot.

Tasting Notes
Medium to thick in consistency and smooth and creamy in texture. The first thing that strikes you is the aroma: just bold, fresh pepper, with a hint of fermented funk. It's fruity and a touch floral, with very little else going on. The taste is immediately fruity, then dry and absolutely murderously hot, searing the tongue. The freshness is still there, though, leading into a deeply warming and slightly salty finish. A biggie, and no mistake.

Other Varieties to Seek Out
Gabko Yellow, Louisiana Gator Blood, Choco (a version of the Red using chocolate-variety peppers), and an Orange Habanero.

Use It For
Another cracking hot wings sauce, or use as a chilli con carne booster.

gabkochilli.hu

HERIOT HOTT
Roasted Pineapple and Yellow Fatalii

While awful for many, the 2020 lockdown was hugely productive for Liam Kerr, who founded Heriot Hott in Edinburgh. Hailing from Lancaster in the north of England, Liam studied biology at the city's Heriot-Watt University, which not only gave him a name for his new brand, but also an understanding of the science behind fermentation, which came in especially helpful with his first pepper mashes. Heriot Hott uses locally grown peppers and as many fresh ingredients as possible. It also follows a sound mantra: that the best hot sauces aren't always the hottest, but the ones packed most full of flavour.

Tasting Notes
Medium in consistency and smooth textured. On opening the bottle you're greeted with an explosion of char-grilled, caramelized pineapple – sweet and really fragrant. On the palate, the pineapple takes centre stage, alongside spicy ginger and ripe banana notes, before the heat develops – a peppery, tingling heat, with a delightful tongue prickle. It's definitely hot, but the sweetness and fruitiness balance it out perfectly.

Origin Edinburgh, Scotland

Chilli Type fatalii

Fire Eater's Heat Rating

))))

Other Varieties to Seek Out
Cherry, Bourbon and Vanilla Barbeque; Yellow Habanero Sweet Chilli; and Charred Peach, Scotch Bonnet and Spiced Rum.

Use It For
Try with a big hunk of mature Cheddar, or in a sandwich with thickly sliced ham. Ham and pineapple, baby. Don't listen to the haters.

heriothott.com

EATEN ALIVE Cacao & Lime Fermented Hot Sauce

Eaten Alive started in 2016 when chefs Pat Bingley and Glyn Gordon were asked to develop a vegan kimchi for a friend's restaurant. That led to them supplying other restaurants and various specialized shops with their fermented products. Now the range includes fermented hot sauces – including the duo's signature Raw Kimchi – plus sauerkraut and other fermented products.

Tasting Notes
A rich chocolate and lime aroma with a lovely underlying smokiness. Thin to medium consistency. The initial taste is a bright tang of limes and vinegar, but there is also a sweetness and a savoury note, which is followed by a velvet-smooth dark chocolate. The smokiness is subtle – as is the heat.

Origin London, England

Chilli Type smoked habanero, cayenne and ancho

Fire Eater's Heat Rating

Other Varieties to Seek Out
Smoked Sriracha, Raw Kimchi, Preserved Lemon.

Use It For
Works great in a marinade and excellent with Mexican-style dishes such as tacos and burritos. If it could do with some lush chocolatey heat, this is worth a try.

eatenalive.co.uk

MAÇARICO Piri-Piri Molho Hot Sauce

Produced by Maçarico, a venerable Portuguese food manufacturer founded in the 1930s, this is arguably the number one Piri Piri sauce in Portugal. It's no boutique, small-batch product, but it's certainly a classic of its type.

Tasting Notes
The aroma is exclusively pure piri piri pepper, concentrated like an essential oil. It has a lovely medium consistency and a deep red colour. The taste is uncomplicated, vibrant pepper with a strong saltiness. Being water-based, it doesn't have the sharpness of many vinegar-based sauces. The heat is mild considering the sauce is 45% peppers, but there's a lovely warmth to the finish.

Origin Portugal

Chilli Type piri piri (bird's eye)

Fire Eater's Heat Rating

Other Varieties to Seek Out
N/A

Use It For
As it's such a simple sauce, it is very versatile. Lovely with chicken, fish, seafood – anything that requires some salty warmth. Also great drizzled on fries!

macarico.pt

KHOO'S HOT SAUCE
The Northern Beacon

Origin Sheffield, England

Chilli Type chocolate naga, red habanero, red cayenne, Dominican red habanero, peach habanero, giant white habanero, 7 pot brain strain, aji mango, peach bhut jolokia, superchilli and bird's eye!

Fire Eater's Heat Rating

Khoo's Hot Sauce was established in 2012 by Alex Khoo, who grows the majority of his own peppers on site in Sheffield. All other ingredients are sourced as locally as possible. Khoo's even smokes its own chipotle peppers. The business received national exposure when it was visited by BBC TV chefs the Hairy Bikers in 2021 and appeared in one of their shows.

Tasting Notes
Is this the record for most chilli pepper types in one sauce? Eleven! The sauce has a lovely and distinctive aroma: a floral scent from the sweet potatoes and mango and then the combination of peppers and some chipotle smoke. The consistency is medium-thick and the flavours are sweet and caramel-like with a hint of butternut squash. There's also a lovely citrussy edge from the lime, lemon and ginger, which gives this a deeply complex flavour. The heat arrives late, but it's a welcome guest: powerful, but not harsh, it fills the mouth and lingers long with a slight smokiness.

Other Varieties to Seek Out
Heavy Smoker, The Bajan, Life's a Peach.

Use It For
Makes a lovely marinade for chicken, as well as a great dipping sauce. See the ribs recipe on page 39, which uses Khoo's Heavy Smoker.

khooshotsauce.co.uk

LEFEVER
Bera

Origin Iceland

Chilli Type habanero

Fire Eater's Heat Rating

A hot sauce from the land of ice? Sounds like an extraordinary paradox, but what an exciting one! LeFever was founded in 2018 by William Óðinn Lefever and his partner Greta Samúelsdóttir in the small fishing village of Djúpivogur, Iceland. Returning from a spell living in Boston to discover only a limited range of hot sauces on offer back home, William took it upon himself to create Iceland's first. After many experiments and abandoned recipes, Bera arrived and five more recipes have followed, all with the same ethos – fresh ingredients, no added sugar and plenty of passion.

Tasting Notes
Immediately fresh and wonderfully tropical, with a heavy mango and banana aroma and flavour developing first. There is a touch of sharp green apple and some herbal notes that coat the tongue – then the heat begins to rise: not hugely bold, but a nice warming subtlety that counterpoints the bold, upfront fruit. Lovely and ripe!

Other Varieties to Seek Out
Alvör, a ginger-heavy recipe; Dreki, a sauce with habanero and reaper peppers; and Jaxl, a Thai-influenced recipe with green Thai chilli.

Use It For
Delicious on a grilled chicken wrap, preferably with a fruit-based salsa.

lefever.is

KAUNAS SAUCE Habanero Peach

Begun in November 2020 by Mantas Urbutis, Kaunas is Lithuania's first dedicated hot sauce company. Urbutis is the owner of the Godo bar, a staple in the city of Kaunas, and quarantine restrictions during the global pandemic allowed him to spend plenty of time in the kitchen developing his concept. Each of his recipes is free of both gluten and artificial preservatives, and his Habanero Peach sauce recently won a prestigious Great Taste award in London.

Tasting Notes
Medium to thick in consistency, with a slightly fleshy texture. The aromas are fresh and a little perfumed, with a pleasant wave of fresh peach and some exotic spiced notes alongside the distinctive habanero aromas. The heat is surprisingly punchy and direct, arriving quickly and sitting alongside a rich sweetness.

Origin Lithuania

Chilli Type habanero

Fire Eater's Heat Rating

))))

Other Varieties to Seek Out
Green Salsa, Sriracha, Habanero & Carrot, Habanero Mango & Sea Buckthorn, and Smoky Chipotle.

Use It For
Great drizzled sparingly on a fresh chicken salad, or mixed with a little oil for a wider, more versatile dressing.

kaunassauce.lt

MR VIKKI'S Hot Stuff Chilli Sauce

Mr Vikki's was founded by award-winning chef Adam Marks in 2005. All the sauces are handmade by Adam in Cumbria, using only fresh ingredients and no preservatives. His range has now expanded to over 30 different products, including excellent chutneys and jams, which have won over 110 awards.

Tasting Notes
The aroma is dominated by the distinctive scotch bonnet pepper and there is a vinegar sharpness but also the sweetness of mango. The consistency on pour is medium with some tiny bits of seed and spice. The rich taste hits with big jalapeño and scotch bonnet flavours, which blend beautifully with the fruity mango. The heat kicks in quickly and is quite fierce on the tongue and continues to build in the finish.

Origin Cumbria, England

Chilli Type scotch bonnet, red jalapeño

Fire Eater's Heat Rating

)))))

Other Varieties to Seek Out
Lime Piri Piri, Lee's Hot Wing Sauce.

Use It For
Excellent with a bacon sandwich.

mrvikkis.co.uk

LONGBOTTOM & CO

The story of Longbottom & Co starts back in 1988 when founders Ed Bathgate and Greg Williams (the latter now a successful Hollywood photographer) first met at school, full of mischievous intent and a shared love of hot sauce and Bloody Marys. Fast forward to 2009 and their first experiments to make, as they say, a 'tastier' hot sauce, rather than head in the direction of the bolder, crazy hots that were emerging at the time. A decade later and, together with co-founder Emma Wykes, they had a business, also turning their hand to developing bottled and canned versions of the perfect Bloody Mary.

Tasting Notes

Fine consistency and smooth texture. The initial aroma is ripe tomato, a hint of herbaceous celery, and a touch of citrus. The flavour is sweet and tomato-heavy, with a nicely balanced savoury spice. The heat is mild, with a slight tingle, bolstered by a cracked black pepper note that lingers on the palate.

Origin London, England

Chilli Type scotch bonnet

Fire Eater's Heat Rating

Other Varieties to Seek Out
N/A

Use It For
Use this in place of ketchup or other tomato-based condiment on chips or potato wedges, or in an utterly delicious bacon sandwich.

longbottom.co

POPPAMIES
Rocoto Sauce

Origin Finland

Chilli Type rocoto

Fire Eater's Heat Rating

'Hot sauces in Finland? That's not a business. It'll never work!' This was the kind of negativity Marko Suksi faced back in 2009 when he considered a life-changing dilemma: follow his dreams of revolutionizing Finland's culinary scene, or continue to work as an engineer for telecoms giant Nokia. Fortunately he didn't listen to the critics and his business has flourished ever since. Poppamies now has a line of 14 sauces, selling over two million bottles a year. Its Rocoto sauce uses the rather unusual rocoto or 'apple pepper', native to Peru and thought to be one of the oldest domesticated peppers in the world.

Tasting Notes
Fine to medium in consistency, with a smooth, glossy texture. A unique, savoury, almost curry-leaf aroma hits first, with fresh lime notes and an earthy spice. The flavours are equally unique: more of the curry-leaf note, a dry, resonant heat and a touch of green apple. The heat is peppery and mouth-coating. Very intriguing and engaging indeed!

Other Varieties to Seek Out
Chipotle and Habanero sauces, a Scorpion sauce (using 57% pepper), and a Sriracha using organic fermented red jalapeños.

Use It For
A great sauce with sweeter-style pizzas, or tacos.

poppamies.fi

PSYCHO JUICE 70% Red Savina

A real treat for the serious chilli-heads out there. Dr. Burnörium's Hot Sauce Emporium is a twisted, fiery and seemingly endless maze of corridors and doorways, each one leading to a different, brutally hot sauce with its own tale. A retail portal, shop and producer, the (bad) doctor has been searing the UK's palates since 2008.

Tasting Notes
A medium consistency, with a smooth texture. The first aroma to arrive is toasted pepper, followed by fresh, fruity, almost candy apple notes. The flavour is bold, dry pepper with a touch of saltiness and a little zesty spice... and that's it. The focus is all on the savina – and it scorches like crazy, bringing almost immediate heat, with a biting bold dryness that lingers and lingers and lingers...

Origin Portsmouth & Bristol, England

Chilli Type red savina habanero

Fire Eater's Heat Rating

ʃʃʃʃʃ

Other Varieties to Seek Out
Chipotle Ghost Pepper, 70% Scorpion Pepper, and 70% Carolina Reaper sauces.

Use It For
Nachos, loaded with cheese.

hotsauceemporium.co.uk

MAISON MARTIN Foudre

Maison Martin is the passion project of three cousins – Jean-Baptiste Martin, Anna Martin (both professional chefs and graduates of the prestigious Ferrandi Paris cooking school) and Benjamin Martin – who all share a love of cuisine and the produce of south-west France. The trio source their peppers (habaneros, naga jolokia and reapers) from local farmers and then ferment them in barrels for three months in their kitchen on the outskirts of Paris, before injecting their culinary magic in the cooking process.

Tasting Notes
Medium-thick in consistency with a slight peppery texture. The open bottle sings fresh red habanero, with luscious fruit and a bit of spicy dryness. The palate is ripe and fresh, with a slight spike of vinegar and beautifully balanced sweetness, with a precise heat that comes alive on the tongue. Very impressive stuff.

Origin Viroflay, Paris, France

Chilli Type habanero

Fire Eater's Heat Rating

Other Varieties to Seek Out
Zéphyr, a barbecue/hot sauce combo; Sirocco, which is more Mexican in style; and a brace of limited edition sauces in partnership with the Gallia brewery in Paris.

Use It For
Grilled lamb, classic steak haché, or as part of a lively salad dressing.

m-martin.fr

RAIJMAKERS HEETMAKERS
Immune Booster

Raijmakers Heetmakers is the brainchild of two brothers, Freek and Stan, with a distinct flair for flavour and design. Despite not having a history of spicy flavours in their native Netherlands, the duo have brought heat and passion to countless customers through their Heatsupply.nl web store, which sells many of the world's best hot sauces. After a while, the brothers decided to develop four distinct recipes of their own, and Raijmakers was born, each sauce combining their favourite peppers with other flavoursome ingredients, such as whiskey, gin, sweet potato and ginger. The bottle and packaging illustrations also perfectly highlight the brothers' elegant, slightly madcap world.

Tasting Notes
Fine and leafy in consistency and texture, the first aromas are fresh, herbal and citrussy, with punchy juniper, green jalapeño and freshly cut lime all jumping out. The flavour is bold and 'green', with layers of jalapeño, tart lime and a lovely sharp but well-balanced heat. Innovative and unlike anything else we've tried!

Origin The Netherlands

Chilli Type jalapeño

Fire Eater's Heat Rating

Other Varieties to Seek Out
Heat Enhancer, with habanero and whiskey; Brain Buzzer, with carolina reaper and ginger; and Tranquilizer, with habanero and sweet potato.

Use It For
A citrus-heavy gin cocktail, such as a Gin Sour, or dashed into a Margarita. Equally delicious on fish tacos or as a dressing for a light tuna salad.

raijmakersheetmakers.com

MEET THE SAUCERER:
Freek Raijmakers, Raijmakers Heetmakers, Netherlands

Pioneers of the hot sauce scene in the Netherlands, Freek Raijmakers and his brother Stan like to explore unusual flavour combinations to match their unconventional approach. They also have perhaps the best, sexiest packaging in hot sauce today!

Tell us about your route into the world of hot sauce...

Our route started with a web store called Heatsupply.nl. We created this so people in Europe could start to enjoy the amazing and hard-to-get hot sauces that are made in the USA and Canada. After one year we felt the urge to create a sauce of our own. Instead of one, we decided to develop four flavours straight away and off we went with Raijmakers Heetmakers.

What do you feel is the most unique aspect about your recipes?

'We are all about flavour over heat' would be a very clichéd answer. To us that's not a very unique selling point of a hot sauce nowadays. Not compromising with local flavour preferences, for example, might be the most unique aspect of our recipes. It's our mission to introduce people to new flavours instead of selling them stuff they already know. For example, our Immune Booster hot sauce has quite a lot of sour notes, such as jalapeño, lime and tomatillo. That might be a flavour profile that not everyone will like, but that's OK. We were convinced about this flavour and people trying it for the first time always get surprised. This goes pretty much for all four flavours.

Why do you think people are so obsessed with the pain/pleasure aspect of hot sauces?

It's the combination of sensation, excitement and flavours. It really adds a new dimension to your food, because it's an experience and not just additional flavours. You will not find that in other products, so a little pain is all worth it.

Have you come across any surprising pairings of foods/drinks with your hot sauces that you love?

Is a grilled peanut butter and banana sandwich with our Brain Buzzer (carolina reaper and ginger) hot sauce surprising enough? Or oysters with our Immune Booster hot sauce?

Can you pick a hot sauce made by someone else that you cannot live without?

It's impossible to only choose one. Queen Majesty Red Habanero & Black Coffee is definitely one of our favourites (see page 64), but Heartbeat from Canada (page 55) also has some amazing hot sauces. Currently we are also hooked on Karma Holé Molé hot sauce (page 59).

Finally, try to sum up Raijmakers in just three words...

Quality. Adventurous. Eye-catching.

ROLESKI SOS Super Hot Habanero!

A stalwart Polish condiment company, family-owned Roleski began producing mayonnaise back in the early 1970s and was one of the first companies to break away from state rule in Poland to become an independent enterprise. Since the 1990s it has been producing a range of condiments and has expanded into hot sauces, from this punchy habanero-based sauce to a bold and intense scorpion pepper-based variety and a teeth-rattling reaper sauce.

Tasting Notes
Very dark and extremely thick in consistency, with a smooth texture. A fruity, sweet spice aroma and flavour emerges first, with stewed apples, woody, dried spices and a dark tamarind note leading into a molasses-heavy and mouth-coating sweetness. Then the heat arrives: peppery and prickly at first, followed by a wave of classic dried habanero notes. It's really dark and rich: think a bolder, close relative of HP brown sauce – with a hidden, red-hot flick knife to slice your tastebuds with.

Origin Poland

Chilli Type habanero

Fire Eater's Heat Rating

))))

Other Varieties to Seek Out
ghost pepper and carolina reaper varieties.

Use It For
Looking for a punchier alternative to spice up your morning fry-up? This is it.

roleski.pl

TUBBY TOM'S Pablo Diablo

Tubby Tom's emerged in 2014 when founder Tom Hughes indulged his passion for food and made his own barbecue sauce. His friends loved it and encouraged him to make more and set up his own brand. Thus, Tubby Tom's was born. The company has gone from strength to strength and now makes more than 70 different products, including sauces, rubs, oils and jams.

Tasting Notes
A fresh subtle smell of onion and jalapeño, with a bright citrus fragrance. The consistency is medium with little pieces of the fruit and veg ingredients for texture. The flavour is both sharp and fruity-sweet, with the limes and peppers dominant. This is balanced by a green vegetable note from the coriander (cilantro) and spinach. The onion and jalapeño linger as the gentle heat emerges. Lovely and subtle – and a real departure from Tubby Tom's other hotter sauces.

Origin Gloucester, England

Chilli Type jalapeño

Fire Eater's Heat Rating

Other Varieties to Seek Out
Korean One, Squealer, Money Shot.

Use It For
The zingy freshness works great with fajitas and tacos. Lovely mixed with mayo for a dip. Smashing on burgers. Would work well in a chicken marinade. Very versatile.

tubbytoms.com

SCARLET FOR YER MA
Original Hot Sauce

Origin Dublin, Ireland

Chilli Type cayenne and smoked morita

Fire Eater's Heat Rating

Founded in 2018 by fabulously ebullient Dubliner Brian O'Neill – part Willy Wonka, part James Joyce – Scarlet sauces are undoubtedly defined by the city they proudly represent. Brian spent months scouring Dublin's artisan food producers and farmers' markets for the freshest ingredients, going through countless iterations of his flagship Original sauce before it was ready to go. The results use naturally smoked peppers, fresh fruit and red wine vinegars and are wonderfully complex, balanced and fun. As Brian says: 'A little nonsense now and then is relished by the wisest men.'

Tasting Notes
Beautifully fresh and balanced, with a medium, smooth consistency: fresh tomatoes, sweet beetroots (beets), and a rich red wine note all hit first – this is a sauce of distinctly deep character. The flavour is sweet, honeyed and fresh tasting, with more of the tomatoes (like a reduced red wine ragù), some dark brown sugar and a hint of smokiness. The heat rises gently: it's moderate and nicely warming, without any burn or prickle and with a very long, lingering fade. Superbly moreish stuff.

Other Varieties to Seek Out
Raspberry Chipotle, Old Fashioned Whiskey, and Molly's Mango & Pineapple.

Use It For
Drizzled across hand-carved ham, with mature cheese and pickled onions. Or mixed in to make some absolutely filthy baked beans.

dublinhotsauce.com

SALSAS SIERRA NEVADA
Infierno

Founded in 2013 by Carlos Carvajal, Salsas y Especias Sierra Nevada (also known as Doctor Salsas) is Spain's first hot sauce company, but its farms also supply the wider sauce industry with fresh peppers, mash, and dried and smoked peppers. Certified organic, it produces a wide range of sauces – as Carlos says, 'from mild to very wild' – and grows jalapeño, habanero and carolina reaper peppers, as well as the lesser-known monkey face yellow, numex shishito and Brazilian starfish varieties.

Tasting Notes
Thick and dark in consistency, with a grainy/seedy texture. The fruitiness is almost tropical at first, with a slight dried fruit sweetness, then the heat hits in a huge dry wave – fierce and unrelenting. There are curry-like spices and spikes of lemon that sizzle the tongue and roof of the mouth too. A real blisterer!

Origin Spain

Chilli Type moruga scorpion, bhut jolokia and carolina reaper

Fire Eater's Heat Rating

Other Varieties to Seek Out
Carolina Reaper sauce, Veneno del Bueno con Mango, Sriracha de Agave, Moruga Madness and Barbacoa.

Use It For
Mix with some olive oil to glaze roasted chicken thighs.

salsasierranevada.com

SINGULARITY SAUCE CO Het Sass Original

A lightbulb moment hit Mark McAulay in 2019 and he realized his life would change forever. As a 20-year veteran of the brand strategy and design world, making tiny amounts of chilli sauce was only ever really a hobby. But when he discovered the secret to fermenting different varieties of pepper and the sheer number of flavours the process can bring, his attention turned fully to his passion, and Singularity's world of 'het sass' was born. Mark's tried-and-tested fermentation process gives his sauces a distinct flavour all of their own, so much so that his moniker as a 'fermentalist' is entirely justified.

Tasting Notes
Thick in consistency and smooth and glossy in texture. The initial aromas are very savoury and spicy, almost curry-leaf like, with a soft note of dry cider and fresh pepper. The palate is a proper explosion of flavour: fresh chilli, an almost orchard-fruit sweetness and a slight tropical note. The balance between sweet and sour is refined nicely. A really distinct and unique sauce.

Origin Aberdeenshire, Scotland

Chilli Type moruga scorpion

Fire Eater's Heat Rating

Other Varieties to Seek Out
Het Sass Bacon, and Buy Ice Cream – an incredible 'dessert hot sauce' with moruga scorpion, habanero, cacao nibs and cherries.

Use It For
This works nicely on a variety of noodle dishes.

singularitysauce.co

SOUTH LONDON SAUCE CO Saint Reatham

Andy Bibey is used to being a man on the move. Originally an artist and tour manager, he spent his time on the road exploring the cuisines of cultures all over the world. In 2020 he took the bold step of setting up South London Sauce Co, alongside acclaimed pop-up pizza company, The Fat Crust, and a new career was born. Andy's flagship sauce, Saint Reatham (a playful take on locals' nickname for Streatham, south London), is his most extreme and packed with big, bold complexity and the classic reaper burn. Andy has also collaborated with scotch whisky firm The Glenlivet to develop a new yellow habanero-based sauce using its Caribbean reserve whiskey.

Tasting Notes
Medium consistency with a fine texture. Huge flavours of ripe tomato, spicy paprika, well-cooked garlic and roasted red pepper. The heat arrives swiftly and brings the whole thing to life: an upfront punchy dry heat that coats the tongue. The complexity of the sauce develops, as does the warmth. A south London triumph!

Origin Streatham, London, England

Chilli Type scotch bonnet, red jalapeño

Fire Eater's Heat Rating

Other Varieties to Seek Out
Mango Jerry, Keeping It South Rojo, Keeping It South Verde, and Peri Wogan.

Use It For
Absolutely brilliant with a pizza and garlic bread.

southlondonsaucecompany.com

WILTSHIRE CHILLI FARM Dark Habanero

Based in the delightful countryside of Melksham, near Bath in south-west England, Wiltshire Chilli Farm is a coming together of horticulturalists, chilli lovers and sauce fanatics. Founded by Jamie Sythes, who started out growing chilli plants on his windowsill and is now one of the UK's most respected chilli farmers, the team grows dozens of varieties, from habaneros to ghosts, reapers and scorpions. The sauces themselves are equally compelling, combining coffee, fresh fruit, cacao and other delicious ingredients.

Tasting Notes

Medium consistency, with a moderately chunky texture. The sauce is very deep in colour and hugely rich in aroma: dark chocolate, sweet muscovado sugar and wild honey, alongside mature red wine. The flavour is instantly bold, with fresh, slightly bitter cacao nibs, lovely sweet dark chocolate and a drying pepper note. The heat arrives as a mid-palate punch – suddenly it's there… and it keeps on coming! The aftertaste is lingering richness and more of the cacao. Superb.

Origin Wiltshire, England

Chilli Type chocolate habanero and chipotle

Fire Eater's Heat Rating

Other Varieties to Seek Out
Golden Bonnet, Fruity Chilli Sauce (with sultanas, apples, ginger and cayenne), and The God Slayer – a Super Hot that features a 6.4 million Scoville chilli oil extract (called an oleoresin).

Use It For
A classic chilli con carne, with added dark chocolate for depth and richness.

justchillies.co.uk

THICCC SAUCE
Bourbon BBQ Sriracha

When Luca Rollini found himself furloughed due to the pandemic, he didn't sit around idly. Making a batch of scotch bonnet sauce at his parents' house, he soon realized he was on to something when it sold out quickly. Word spread and, before he knew it, Thiccc was born, driven by a thirst for adventure in flavour and a desire to find the best, most inventive collaborative partners. Rollini had previously spent months travelling across the USA and saw a synergy between small-batch sauces and craft beer. Today Thiccc works with a range of craft breweries across the UK, which are equally pushing the boundaries with unusual ingredients. Think mole sauces with smoked jalapeño, cooked in craft stout, with maple syrup and cinnamon; a breakfast pancake-influenced sauce with red berries, reaper peppers, vanilla and beer; and, in our opinion, his true masterpiece – this Maker's Mark bourbon-infused BBQ Sriracha, developed with Adam Layton from UK artisan restaurant group Honest Burgers.

Tasting Notes
Sticky, with a medium-thick consistency. The first aromas are heavenly: deep, rich smoke, hickory and char-grilled meat, with a potent, sweet tomato and muscovado sugar note. The flavour is intense: sweet then tangy, with a blast of smoke (think vanilla tobacco) leading into a black pepper dryness. The heat then arrives: moderate, but warming and tantalizing at the back of the throat. It lingers wonderfully before returning to a last-embers-of-a-bonfire note. Unique and absolutely moreish.

Origin Leeds, England

Chilli Type red jalapeño and chipotle

Fire Eater's Heat Rating

Other Varieties to Seek Out
Carolina Gold Honey Mustard BBQ, Seoul Food Korean Gochujang, and Mindflayer Dill Pickle Jalapeño CBD Infused Hot Sauce.

Use It For
Properly filthy baby back ribs – and makes maybe the best barbecue baked beans ever.

thicccsauce.com

WHITE WHALE SAUCES
Limonhello

White Whale might never have existed if founder Tom Vermeulen had been more honest with his wife-to-be! Instead a simple white lie turned into a life-changing moment. Tom, a man with some culinary experience but little knowledge of hot peppers, decided to impress his girlfriend, who is of Turkish/Palestinian descent, by biting into a habanero – an old Turkish practice if someone is caught telling fibs. While not pleasant, the experience triggered the inevitable endorphin rush and prompted the couple to explore sauce making to a serious level, learning about fermentation and bringing together unusual ingredients such as kiwi fruit and hoppy beer. Limonhello uses the madame jeanette pepper, which is native to Suriname and related to the habanero.

Tasting Notes
Very thick in consistency and fleshy in texture. The initial aromas are fresh, zingy and fruity, with distinct lemon zest notes and rich spices, alongside some diced apple. The flavours are sweet and fruity, with an explosion of lemon that leads to a zesty kick. The heat is medium – hot and creeping with a nicely balanced warmth that has lingering depth, highlighting the zestiness.

Origin Eindhoven, Netherlands

Chilli Type jalapeño and madame jeanette

Fire Eater's Heat Rating

Other Varieties to Seek Out
Electric Ocean, with madame jeanette pepper and beer, and Teqiwi, with roasted green jalapeño, kiwi and tequila.

Use It For
Fancy spicing up a lemon sorbet or creamy posset? This tastes fabulous drizzled on top.

whitewhalesauces.nl

MIDDLE & FAR EAST

7R7R Caribbean Red & Apples

'7r7r' is the literal English representation of an Arabic word used to describe the feeling when eating spicy food. The company was founded in 2018 by Michel Moukarzel, whose passion for hot food started at an early age when he ate his grandfather's pepper paste, made using chillies from his garden. Lebanon isn't particularly well known for super-hot cuisine, so Michel decided to explore the possibilities of cultivating his own peppers to create a decidedly spicy but not 'brutal' sauce. He initially grew 50 plants, including scotch bonnet, habanero, ghost and some milder indigenous Lebanese varieties. Fast forward to today and he has over 1,000 plants growing and a range of three sauces, each with their own personality.

Tasting Notes
Thick in consistency, with a soft texture. The first aromas are a lovely mix of apple, garlic, sautéed onion and fresh, ripe pepper – the unmistakable scotch bonnet. It quickly coats the palate with soft, spicy stewed apple, more of the sautéed onion and a prickly, tingly bite of the peppers that arrives quickly and starts to fade after a few seconds into a pleasant warmth. Fruity and nicely balanced.

Origin Ain Aar, Lebanon

Chilli Type scotch bonnet

Fire Eater's Heat Rating

)))

Other Varieties to Seek Out
Ghosts & Carrots, Red Hab & Sweet Chili.

Use It For
A traditional chicken shawarma wrap.

@7r7r.hotsauce on Instagram

LINGHAM'S
Original Chilli Sauce

Origin Malaysia

Chilli Type unknown

Fire Eater's Heat Rating

A bona fide classic and no mistake. The story of Lingham's goes back to 1908 when Mr Lingam, of Indian descent, emigrated to Penang in Malaysia. Missing his home cuisine, he created a hot sauce that went down a storm with local British expatriates. Lingam adapted the name to make it sound more British (adding an 'h') and Lingham's was born. The simple recipe of sugar, chilli peppers, salt and vinegar has proved popular with several prominent members of the British royal family.

Tasting Notes
Thick and sticky in consistency, with a slightly course texture. The sauce is initially vinegar led on the nose, with an underlying chilli sweetness. The first taste is also sweet: akin to a traditional sweet chilli sauce, with a moderate heat and flavours of fresh green apple and a touch of dried pepper.

Other Varieties to Seek Out
Lingham's Garlic Chilli Sauce, Extra Hot Chilli Sauce, Ginger Garlic Chilli Sauce, and a Sriracha.

Use It For
Particularly nice on tiger prawns (shrimp) in a tossed salad or with grilled lobster.

linghams.uk

MELLOW HABANERO
Yuzu Heaven

For Taku Kondo, the humble habanero is as much a medium for creating art as it is a way of life and perfect business partner. His story started in 2001, when he moved from Shibuya in Tokyo, where he ran a successful curry food truck, to the idyllic surroundings of Ishigaki island in Okinawa. After a friend gave him a single habanero, Taku's life changed forever: he started growing his own chillies and developing sauces using plants descended from that original habanero. His pepper wisdom has since become the stuff of legend and, now based in Osaka, his place as arguably Japan's most exciting hot-sauce maker is sealed, winning first prize at the World Hot Sauce Awards and collaborating with New York's Heatonist (see page 56) on his Yuzu Heaven recipe.

Tasting Notes
Medium-thick in consistency, with a smooth texture. The freshness immediately leaps from the bottle: ripe, fruity yellow habaneros with a background note of tropical, sweet mango and a touch of yuzu sharpness. On the palate you have rich, luscious, plump fresh habanero – ripe, sweet, then dry, with a intense heat developing. The punch is there and it lasts, but so does the freshness, with the sweetness also returning. Wonderfully hot, but heavenly as hell at the same time.

Origin Japan

Chilli Type habanero

Fire Eater's Heat Rating

Other Varieties to Seek Out
Mellow Habanero Mild, Extra, Smoky, and Habanero Heaven versions.

Use It For
Makes for an incredibly fresh marinade for a chicken salad and also good added into a fruit-based salsa.

mellowhabanero.myshopify.com

SHARK BRAND
Sriracha Chili Sauce

Origin Thailand

Chilli Type unspecified Thai peppers

Fire Eater's Heat Rating

Which brand can truly lay claim to being the most authentic Sriracha sauce? Many would point to David Tran's Huy Fong (see page 58), but some say Shark fits the bill. Produced by the Kosol-Ampa company, it was first introduced over 70 years ago when its founders left China for the Chonburi province of Thailand with the dream of creating a sauce brand. Today the company remains in family ownership and the recipe is unchanged, using only locally grown ingredients. Introduced into the USA in 1983, it has since acquired cult status, with celebrity chefs such as American Andy Ricker, known for his expertise in Thai cuisine, heaping praise upon it.

Tasting Notes
Fine to medium and silky consistency. The aromas are full and fresh, with stewed peppers and fruity tomato alongside a sharp-but-pleasant vinegar note. The sauce is vibrant and sweet on the palate, with a rich, deep flavour of pepper and a backbone of well-cooked garlic that doesn't overpower. The heat is restrained and warming, never overstepping the mark. Shark is a very pleasant sauce that doesn't bite too hard...

Other Varieties to Seek Out
Seagull Brand reduced sugar and Swallow Brand strong versions.

Use It For
Dim sum and pork with egg-fried rice. The finer consistency makes it easy to use as a base for other sauces and marinades.

kosolampa.com

DUA BELIBIS Chilli Sauce

A well-known Indonesian brand of hot sauce, Dua Belibis, or 'Two Ducks', from north Jakarta is popular as a dipping sauce with dishes such as *mie udang* (spicy noodles with prawns) and as an accompaniment to fried chicken and other local specialties.

Tasting Notes
Medium consistency with a glossy texture. Initial aroma of well-cooked tomatoes, grilled peppers and fried garlic. The palate is savoury with a salty/umami note, leading to a sweetness and lingering chilli bite that develops into a black pepper-like prickle on the tongue. The heat is lingering and dry.

Origin Indonesia

Chilli Type unknown

Fire Eater's Heat Rating

Other Varieties to Seek Out
N/A

Use It For
Fresh shellfish, such as prawns (jumbo shrimp) or crayfish.

duabelibis.co.id

AMOY Chilli Sauce

Amoy is a name familiar to many because of its popular soy sauce brand, an international market leader. Founded in 1908, the company first bottled its soy sauce in Xiamen, China, before moving production to Hong Kong in 1928 and developing a vast range of other condiments, including chilli and oyster sauces and a number of marinades. Its sweet chilli sauce has been widely adopted as a dipping sauce in Chinese restaurants across Europe and North America, although this pure chilli sauce is less well known.

Tasting Notes
Very thick consistency, with a coarse texture. The initial aromas are full-on roasted peppers, with touches of vinegar and sweet, fresh, almost orchard fruit. The flavour is very savoury, with dried chilli, a distinct umami/mushroom note and a light undertone of rice vinegar. The heat is mild and swift on the palate.

Origin Hong Kong

Chilli Type unknown

Fire Eater's Heat Rating

Other Varieties to Seek Out
Amoy Sweet Chilli Sauce, Toban Chilli Bean Sauce.

Use It For
Stir into dishes such as pan-fried noodles or add to a traditional pork loin hot and sour soup.

amoy.com

PICO
Naga Ghost Pepper Sauce

Origin Mumbai, India

Chilli Type ghost pepper

Fire Eater's Heat Rating

Pico was started as part of the Nilgai Foods brand in 2015 by London-based Arjun Gadkari. He wanted to create authentic products that reflected contemporary Indian food culture for the British market. The sauces are all made in Mumbai and are now sold in India, Singapore, the UK and the USA.

Tasting Notes
A nice fruity scent from the ghost pepper hits the nose upon opening the bottle, along with strong garlic and spice notes. The consistency is smooth to medium. A mix of fruity pepper, saltiness and Indian spice mix are the first flavours to arrive, making it very savoury, with no real sweetness or vinegar notes. Then the fierce heat kicks in – a great burn that fills the mouth and lasts.

Other Varieties to Seek Out
Maha Green Chilli Sauce, Konkan Mango Chilli Sauce.

Use It For
Blended nicely with mayo to temper the heat, it's great in a burger. Works brilliantly with Indian street food, too.

picosauces.com

YEO'S Singapore Chilli Sauce

Founded by Yeo Keng Lian, the Yeo company can trace its history back over 120 years to the city of Zhangzhou in the Fujian province of China. The Yeo family moved to Singapore in the 1930s and expanded its repertoire from a popular soy sauce into a range encompassing chilli sauces, sesame oils and instant noodles, all of which became part of the fabric of Singapore cuisine. Today the business exports its ever-popular sauces all over the world and remains a firm favourite in restaurants, store cupboards and fridges across Singapore and Malaysia.

Tasting Notes
Thick, ketchup-like consistency, with a smooth texture. The aroma is full of lemongrass, ginger, warming spices and fresh chillies, with a bold, spicy and very complex flavour, including more ginger, a touch of garlic, a slightly smoky pepper note and warming fresh chilli. The heat rises up on the palate and is warming and pleasant. A sauce unlike anything else in this book!

Origin China/Singapore

Chilli Type unknown

Fire Eater's Heat Rating

Other Varieties to Seek Out
Hot Chilli Sauce, Sweet Chilli Sauce.

Use It For
Malaysian-style pork meatballs, chicken and aubergine (eggplant) stir fry, and Thai-spicy king prawn (shrimp) salad.

yeos-europe.com

YUZUSCO Hot Yuzu Sauce

The Yuzusco brand was created by Takahashi Shoten, a sake brewer, in 1946, and has diversified into a number of traditional and artisanal Japanese delicacies, including scallops, sea mushrooms and herring roe, all pickled in sake lees (a fruity yeast product left after the production of sake rice wine). With the distinguishing lead flavour of yuzu, the hugely popular Japanese citrus fruit, its sauces offer a distinct freshness.

Tasting Notes
Fine consistency with a light herbaceous texture. Very bright and citrus-led on the nose, with the zingy freshness of yuzu (think lime zest and lemongrass aromas) and touches of fresh mint and sake wine. The flavour is initially a little salty, leading into more yuzu freshness, some green herbs and a rising heat – gentle at first, then nicely warming and piquant.

Origin Yanagawa City, Japan

Chilli Type unknown

Fire Eater's Heat Rating

Other Varieties to Seek Out
Yuzusco Red (with more pepper heat) and Ginger varieties.

Use It For
The freshness and vibrancy work well in cocktails such as a Japanese whisky highball. It also makes a superb dipping sauce for maki rolls and tuna sashimi.

yuzusco.com

FLYING GOOSE Sriracha Hot Chilli Sauce

The huge success of Huy Fong 'Rooster' Sriracha (see page 58) has clearly manifested 'a rising tide floats all boats' scenario, with myriad similar-looking brands cropping up since it appeared. But it would be unfair to describe all these sauces as mere copycats. Flying Goose's packaging may bear a striking resemblance to the Rooster's but it has a distinct profile all of its own. Introduced in 1999, this Sriracha Hot Chilli Sauce uses peppers from Thai farmsteads and has a high chilli content (61%), so expect it to taste like it should: the real deal.

Tasting Notes
Medium consistency with a silky, glossy and slightly sticky texture. The first notes are a complex combo of umami-esque savoury/saltiness and a touch of drying funkiness, followed by a spicy, ripe fruitiness. The heat arrives swiftly and is well-rounded and prickly, leading into white pepper notes and a delicious red berry fruitiness.

Origin Thailand

Chilli Type unknown

Fire Eater's Heat Rating

Other Varieties to Seek Out
Sriracha Super Hot, Sriracha Blackout, Sriracha Smokey, and Sriracha Black Pepper.

Use It For
An undisputed classic to accompany meals such as chicken noodle salads, poke bowls and pan-fried salmon and sticky rice.

flyinggoosebrand.com

NAAGIN INDIAN HOT SAUCE The Original

Naagin was founded in 2020 by Mikhel Rajani, Kshitij Neelakantan and Arjun Rastogi. Although India is home to one of the world's great styles of spicy cuisine, the country's number one hot sauce was an American product made with chillies from Mexico! Naagin set out to change that.

Tasting Notes

A smooth medium-thick consistency with an aroma of gentle spicy onion, garlic and tomato. The taste is sweet tangy tomato and onion, balanced nicely with garlic, before the distinctive Indian chilli notes reveal themselves. A dry, slightly sour, earthy burn that is quite unique.

Origin Mumbai, India

Chilli Type sankeshwari and bhavnagri

Fire Eater's Heat Rating

Other Varieties to Seek Out
Smoky Bhoot, Kantha Bomb.

Use It For
Great with Indian street food snacks such as bhajis and samosas, but versatile enough to be used on anything in place of a good tomato ketchup.

naaginsauce.com

YOYO LAOS SAUCE
Ginger Chilli Sauce

Yoyo Laos Sauce was founded by the amazing Hatsadee Xayavongchanch, aka Yoyo, in 2020. She moved to the UK from Laos in 2015 and found that everyone fell in love with her homemade sauces when she took them to barbecues and parties. This gave her the idea and confidence to start the company and, before long, a range of sauces was born. The brand also has an admirable charitable angle: Laos is one of the most bombed countries in the world, a consequence of the Vietnam War, and unexploded bombs still affect rural communities today. Ten pence from every bottle of Yoyo sauce sold goes to the Mines Advisory Group charity, which helps to make the country a safer place to live.

Tasting Notes
Thick consistency, with a nicely textured chunkiness from the ginger and pepper. On the nose, the aromas are full of lovely subtle ginger and lime. If you enjoy the flavours of south-east Asian food, this sauce will immediately transport you there, with big doses of pickled ginger, salty lime and soothing coconut. The sweet, sour and saltiness is brilliantly balanced and the warm chilli burn is long and medium-hot, but not jarring.

Origin Laos (via Halifax, England)

Chilli Type bird's eye red and green

Fire Eater's Heat Rating

Other Varieties to Seek Out
Lan Xang Sauce, Luang Prabang Special Sauce.

Use It For
Noodle and rice dishes, chicken noodle soup, or spoon directly into mouth!

yoyolaossauce.co.uk

MEET THE SAUCERER:

Hatsadee 'Yoyo' Xayavongchanch, Yoyo Sauces, Laos (via the UK)

From Laos via Yorkshire, Yoyo sauces are original, playful and full-flavoured, with a unique twist. Founder Yoyo reveals the secrets behind some of her most inventive creations.

Tell us about your route into the world of hot sauce. Was it love at first bite or something else that made you fall head over heels for it?

I'm originally from Laos and in my country we eat a lot of fresh vegetables, fish and meat, which are frequently served with sticky rice and *jeow*, which is our – often spicy – dipping sauce. I love to cook for friends and family, and my 'Laos sauce' would be a favourite. In 2020 when I was struggling to find work, my husband and I decided to turn what was a hobby into a business, and here we are nearly three years later with Yoyo Laos Sauce winning awards and selling all over the UK and beyond!

What's the secret behind a great hot sauce?
I think the best hot sauces use fresh ingredients. Buying the best you can makes a real difference as well as choosing all-natural ingredients with no artificial preservatives. Maintaining the consistency with the recipe when scaling up is important, too. Often the quality can drop in the move from handmade small batch to a product produced in larger quantities. Quality will always win out.

Is the chilli pepper's flavour as important as the heat in the hot sauces that you make?

Yes, with my sauces I have always aimed to prioritize flavour over heat. Some hot sauces I find are rather flavourless, particularly those using chilli extract that are really more of an endurance than enjoyable. There are some chilli peppers that provide good levels of heat but are really flavoursome. More recently I've been using scotch bonnet peppers, which have a lovely sweet fruitiness to them.

Who or what has been your biggest influence in creating the successful recipes you have worked on?

My heritage is my biggest influence. Food from Laos is relatively unknown compared with that of neighbouring countries, such as Thailand and Vietnam, but there are many wonderful dishes using herbs and spices that I'd love to inspire interest in, to raise awareness of Laotian food, that have also inspired my sauces.

Do you have a favourite food/drink recipe that uses your hot sauce?

I have two favourites, both are simple dishes. The first is a traditional Laotian dish of grilled belly pork or beef and sticky rice – I just love to dip the pork and rice in my original Yoyo Laos Sauce. The second would be king prawns (jumbo shrimp) salad. My sauce is so good with seafood. I really enjoy a freshly made salad – adding the sauce as a dressing is a perfect summer meal.

Can you pick a hot sauce made by someone else that you cannot live without?

This is easy to answer for me – although it's not quite a sauce, but it's pretty close! It would be Mr Vikki's Tamarind Chipotle Chutney, which is just wonderful (see page 129).

Finally, try to sum up Yoyo Laos Sauce in just three words...

Authentic, fresh, moreish.

AUSTRALASIA

CULLEY'S Fiery Sriracha No.5

New Zealand's Culley's sauces have a lineage that stretches all the way back to 1975. The man behind them, chef Chris Cullen, has endeavoured to push the boundaries of world-beating flavour in every recipe, exploring a range of peppers along the way, from green habanero through to the reaper, with each sauce expressing its heat intensity in numerical form on the front. In recent years, Culley's has also expanded to become a retail portal for other hot sauces.

Tasting Notes
Medium consistency and smooth in texture. A very aromatic and spicy fermented pepper note hits first, with a complex body of fried garlic, sweet molasses and tart wine vinegar. The flavour is equally as bold, with the peppers stepping up the intensity, alongside a nicely balanced touch of garlic. The heat is very punchy indeed, making for a definite upgrade on more traditional Sriracha-style sauces.

Origin New Zealand

Chilli Type red jalapeño

Fire Eater's Heat Rating

))))

Other Varieties to Seek Out
Verde Green Chile No.3, Tropical Caribbean No.7, and Farkin' Hell It's Hot No. 12.

Use It For
Jackfruit or fish tacos.

culleys.co.nz

DIEMEN'S
Stinger Hot Sauce

Origin New South Wales, Australia

Chilli Type red cayenne, red habanero

Fire Eater's Heat Rating

As children, brothers Doug and Derrick Compeau were hooked on Frank's classic RedHot sauce (see page 53). Their addiction eventually led them to setting up Diemen's in 2014 with marketing expert Richard Hack and artist Reece Hobbins. The company name comes from the Tasmanian diemen mountain pepper berry – a unique ingredient in its sauce recipes.

Tasting Notes
A medium consistency and a tangy, spicy vinegar aroma, with the habanero pepper poking its piquancy through early on. There is a rich depth of flavour and earthiness to the sauce, as well as an underlying hot citrus-sweetness, perhaps from the diemen pepper berry. The vinegar is pronounced but not overbearing. The heat builds and is strong but pleasant and there is a distinctive aftertaste – maybe that diemen pepper berry again?

Other Varieties to Seek Out
Original and Inferno.

Use It For
A great burger sauce, or drizzled on grilled lamb chops.

diemens.com.au

FIRE DRAGON CHILLIES
New Zealand Green

Inspired by encounters with spicy food and chillies during extensive travels around Asia and Central and South America in the early 2000s, Clint Meyer began growing his own chillies and making sauces in his native New Zealand. Fire Dragon Chillies was born in 2008 and Clint's range of hot goods now includes more than a dozen sauce varieties, plus chilli chocolate, chilli salt and fresh chillies and seeds. All his chillies are proudly organic, ingredients are locally sourced, and the sauces are all preservative and additive free.

Tasting Notes
An interesting and unusual 'green' aroma, probably from the chilli peppers, but with hints of citrus and radishy wasabi. The consistency is medium but with pieces of fresh ingredients adding texture. The taste is fresh, with lemon and lime notes, slightly fruity from the chillies, but also quite peppery with a subtle vinegar note. The heat is almost instant and persists along with a lemony aftertaste.

Origin Aotearoa, New Zealand

Chilli Type jalapeño and super hots

Fire Eater's Heat Rating

Other Varieties to Seek Out
Deadly Chilli Sauce, Dragons Fury, Smoky Dragon Sh!thot Chipotle.

Use It For
Great with fish and even with sushi. Works well with south-east Asian-style dishes such as green curry or pho.

firedragonchillies.co.nz

MEET THE SAUCERER:
Clint Meyer, Fire Dragon Chillies, New Zealand

One of New Zealand's hot sauce hot shots, Clint Meyer explains how travelling was one of the greatest influences on his recipes.

Tell us about your route into the world of hot sauce. Was it love at first bite or did something else make you fall head over heels for it?

I've always loved spicy food for as long as I can remember. For some reason, after a few drinks had gone down at many of the 21st birthdays I attended, someone would bring around a bowl of chillies to munch on. The endorphin rush you get from eating a raw chilli was a buzz for me and now I have chilli with just about every meal. I made my first hot sauce while travelling/working in Canada in 2005. It was a deadly wing sauce – and from there I was totally hooked on hot sauces.

What's the secret behind a great hot sauce?
Good-quality chillies and ingredients. Simple recipes using local and organic produce can turn into some amazing hot sauces.

Is the chilli pepper's flavour as important as the heat in the hot sauces that you make?

Flavour is important but so is the heat, as we try to make our sauces as hot as possible without losing the flavour of the chillies and ingredients. There are so many amazing flavours in different chilli cultivars that the possibilities of hot sauces are endless.

Who or what has been your biggest influence in creating the successful recipes you have worked on?

Probably travelling through Central America had the biggest influence as there was a lot to try. One sauce that blew my mind was a Marie Sharp's Habanero Pepper Sauce with carrot (see page 90). That became my daily go-to hot sauce while travelling through Guatemala. A lot of fresh chillies were consumed on that trip, too!

Any brilliant and surprising pairings of foods/drinks with hot sauces that you've come across?

To me, chilli goes with everything except cereal, which I don't eat very often! I do love a good chilli beer. There's been quite a few brewers in NZ making different versions over the years, with each one being unique: some warm and some flaming hot. You either love a chilli beer or hate it!

Can you pick a hot sauce made by someone else that you cannot live without?

It would have to be Wild West Worcester Blacksauce. A must for breakfast, along with some of our Super Hot chilli salt.

Finally, try to sum up Fire Dragon Chillies in just three words...

Hot. As. F**k!

BUNSTERS
Original Hot Sauce

Origin Victoria, Australia

Chilli Type bird's eye

Fire Eater's Heat Rating

Founded in 2012 by Renae Bunster, a former journalist who was inspired to make her own hot sauce after a trip to Mexico and Central America. She began selling it at markets and in 2015 decided to make a sauce 'so hot that nobody would be able to eat it', jokingly naming it 'Shit the Bed'. A photo of the sauce bottle went viral and orders flooded in from Australia and the USA. The business has grown rapidly and now includes a line of eight different sauces, peanut butter, and even ready-to-drink cocktails.

Tasting Notes
The consistency is medium, with a thick texture of vegetables and spices. The complex aroma is primarily of tomatoes, red peppers and onion, alongside more exotic notes of lime, coconut and ginger. The taste is well balanced with all ingredients discernible – savoury, fruity, salty and sweet, with ginger, bell peppers, onion and lime. No one ingredient dominates. The heat from the bird's eye peppers is medium and reveals itself after the main flavours have subsided.

Other Varieties to Seek Out
Shit the Bed, Salami Sauce, Black Label.

Use It For
A great all-rounder, fantastic with eggs, burgers, pizzas and French fries.

bunstersworldwide.com

MELBOURNE HOT SAUCE Habanero & Mango

Chef Richard Nelson founded Melbourne Hot Sauce in 2013 with the aim of creating a range of versatile sauces that can be used as condiments but also dressings, marinades and dips. All the sauces are proudly made from natural ingredients, with no preservatives, additives or thickeners.

Tasting Notes

A smooth to medium consistency. A clean tangy smell of fruity tropical mango and vinegar, plus the unmistakable aroma of habanero pepper. The taste highlights a simple sauce of few ingredients but is clean, and each component is distinct. The sweet mango is enhanced by orange and pungent habanero, with a background hint of cardamom. The heat is upfront and lingers long with the mango flavour persisting alongside the burn.

Origin Melbourne, Australia

Chilli Type habanero

Fire Eater's Heat Rating

))))

**Other Varieties
to Seek Out**
Reaper Whisky BBQ,
Hop Smoked Jalapeño,
Tomatillo & Jalapeño.

Use It For
Perfect to give Indian food a sweet kick and fantastic in a spicy dressing to go with prawn (shrimp) salad.

melbournehotsauce.com

THE FIRE EATER'S QUICK-GLANCE GUIDE

)

Amoy Chilli Sauce (Hong Kong, page 153)
Chilli of the Valley Pasilla Queen of the Dessert (Wales, page 113)
Firelli Italian Hot Sauce (Italy, page 122)
La Preferida Louisiana-Style Hot Sauce (USA, page 60)
Maratá Gota Picante Molho de Pimenta Verde (Brazil, page 88)
Mendez Hot Sauce (Brazil, page 99)
Texas Pete Original (USA, page 73)
Tubby Tom's Pablo Diablo (England, page 138)

))

Búfalo Salsa Picante Clásica (Mexico, page 43)
Crystal Hot Sauce (USA, page 48)
Devil Dog Sauces Jalapeño & Pineapple (England, page 119)
Dirty Dick's Hot Sauce (USA, page 45)
Don Gaucho Chimichurri Picante (Argentina, page 85)
Dr Trouble Double Oak Smoked Chilli (Zimbabwe, page 107)
Eaten Alive Cacao & Lime Fermented Hot Sauce (England, page 126)
Encona West Indian Original Hot Pepper Sauce (Jamaica, page 81)

Huichol Salsa Picante (Mexico, page 45)
Huy Fong 'Rooster' Sriracha (USA, page 58)
La Meridana Papaya Habanero (Mexico, page 60)
LeFever Bera (Iceland, page 128)
Légal Hot Sauce Medium (Brazil, page 86)
Lingham's Original Chilli Sauce (Malaysia, page 149)
Longbottom & Co (England, page 130)
Lottie's Original Barbados Recipe Hot Pepper Sauce (Barbados, page 88)
Maçarico Piri-Piri Molho Hot Sauce (Portugal, page 126)
Raijmakers Heetmakers Immune Booster (Netherlands, page 135)
Scarlet for Yer Ma Original Hot Sauce (Ireland, page 139)
Shark Brand Sriracha Chili Sauce (Thailand, page 152)
Tabasco Original (USA, page 68)
Tapatío Salsa Picante (USA, page 61)
Valentina Salsa Picante (Mexico, page 72)
Yeo's Singapore Chilli Sauce (China/Singapore, page 155)
Yuzusco Hot Yuzu Sauce (Japan, page 155)

)))

Amazon Pepper Co Green Amazon (Colombia, page 80)
Bunsters Original Hot Sauce (Australia, page 168)
Chika Chika Fire Roasted Tamarind Chilli (Kenya, page 105)
Cholula Original (Mexico, page 46)
Chorrito Sauce Co Hot Honey & Bourbon (Scotland, page 114)
Crooked Pickle Co Nero Black Pepper Hot Sauce (England, page 122)
Dua Belibis Chilli Sauce (Indonesia, page 153)
D'Vanya's Junkanoo Hot Pepper Sauce (Bahamas, page 85)
Flying Goose Sriracha Hot Chilli Sauce (Thailand, page 156)
Frank's RedHot Original (USA, page 53)
Howler Monkey Original (USA, page 52)
KanKun Mexican Habanero Sauce (Mexico, page 49)
Matouk's Trinidad Hot Sauce (Trinidad and Tobago, page 89)
Naagin Indian Hot Sauce The Original (India, page 157)
Pickapeppa Hot Mango Sauce (Jamaica, page 97)

Queen Majesty Scotch Bonnet & Ginger Hot Sauce (USA, page 64)

Secret Aardvark Habanero (USA, page 67)

Singularity Sauce Co Het Sass Original (Scotland, page 142)

Thiccc Sauce Bourbon BBQ Sriracha (England, page 144)

Torchbearer Son of Zombie (USA, page 75)

White Whale Sauces Limonhello (Netherlands, page 147)

Windmill Products Hot Pepper Sauce (Barbados, page 100)

Yellowbird Blue Agave Sriracha (USA, page 77)

Yoyo Laos Sauce Ginger Chilli Sauce (Laos, page 158)

7R7R Caribbean Red & Apples (Lebanon, page 148)

𝄋𝄋

Aunt May's Bajan Pepper Sauce (Barbados, page 83)

Baron West Indian Hot Sauce (St Lucia, page 84)

Black Mamba Cayenne Chilli Sauce (Eswatini, page 102)

Blair's Original Death Sauce (USA, page 42)

Condimaniac Smokey Dragon (England, page 112)

Culley's Fiery Sriracha No.5 (New Zealand, page 162)

Dawson's Original Hot (Canada, page 43)

Diemen's Stinger Hot Sauce (Australia, page 163)

El Yucateco Salsa Picante Roja de Chile Habanero (Mexico, page 79)

Fire Dragon Chillies New Zealand Green (New Zealand, page 164)

Heartbeat Hot Sauce Co Scorpion Picante (Canada, page 55)

Heartbreaking Dawns 1841 Ghost Pepper Hot Sauce (USA, page 52)

Heriot Hott Roasted Pineapple and Yellow Fatalii (Scotland, page 124)

Kaunas Sauce Habanero Peach (Lithuania, page 129)

Le Phare du Cap Bon Harissa (Tunisia, page 110)

Maison Martin Foudre (France, page 133)

Marie Sharp's Habanero Pepper Sauce (Belize, page 90)

Melbourne Hot Sauce Habanero & Mango (Australia, page 169)

Mellow Habanero Yuzu Heaven (Japan, page 151)

Nali Hot (Malawi, page 104)

Poppamies Rocoto Sauce (Finland, page 132)

Roleski SOS Super Hot Habanero! (Poland, page 138)

Small Axe Peppers Ghost Pepper Hot Sauce (USA, page 69)

Walkerswood Scotch Bonnet Pepper Sauce (Jamaica, page 89)

𝄋𝄋𝄋

Adoboloco Hamajang (USA, page 41)

CaJohns Memento Mori (USA, page 44)

Chief Scorpion Pepper Sauce (Trinidad and Tobago, page 84)

Crazy Bastard Ghost Pepper & Mango (Germany, page 117)

Dave's Gourmet Insanity Sauce (USA, page 51)

Gabko Hot Pepper Sauce Red (Hungary, page 123)

Hellfire Fear This! (USA, page 49)

Johnny Hexburg Chocolate Bhutlah (South Africa, page 103)

Karma Sauce Cherry Bomb (USA, page 59)

Khoo's Hot Sauce The Northern Beacon (England, page 127)

Mr Vikki's Hot Stuff Chilli Sauce (England, page 129)

Pico Naga Ghost Pepper Sauce (India, page 154)

Psycho Juice 70% Red Savina (England, page 133)

PuckerButt Pepper Company The Reaper (USA, page 61)

Ricante Fire Melons (Costa Rica, page 98)

Salsas Sierra Nevada Infierno (Spain, page 140)

South London Sauce Co Saint Reatham (England, page 142)

Wiltshire Chilli Farm Dark Habanero (England, page 143)

Heatonist The Last Dab Apollo (USA, page 56)

BURN AFTER READING

Thanks for making it to the end! Here you'll find retailers, events, books and websites we've selected to help further your love of hot sauces and the world of chilli peppers.

Hot Sauce Retailers

UK
Bauce Brothers baucebrothers.com
ChilliCult chillicult.co.uk
Chilli Island chilliisland.co.uk
Chilli Shop Leeds facebook.com/
ChilliShopLeedsMerrionCentre
Dr Burnorium's Hot Sauce Emporium
hotsauceemporium.co.uk
Flaming Licks flaminglicks.com
Hop Burns & Black hopburnsblack.co.uk
Hot-Headz hot-headz.com
Mexgrocer mexgrocer.co.uk
Mexican Mama mexican-mama.com
Scorchio scorchio.co.uk
Some Like It Hot. Shop
somelikeithot.shop

Ireland
Stinky & Scorchy stinkyandscorchy.ie

US/Canada
Chilly Chiles chillychiles.com
Fuego Box fuegobox.com
Heat Hot Sauce Shop heathotsauce.com
Heatonist heatonist.com
Hotlicks hotlickssauces.com
Hotsauce.com
iBurn iburn.com
Peppers.com
Pepper Palace pepperpalace.com
Pepperworld pepperworldhotshop.com
Tears of Joy tearsofjoysauces.com
United Sauces unitedsauces.com

Germany
Pepperworld pepperworldhotshop.com

France
Force & Saveur forceetsaveur.com
Sauce Piquante sauce-piquante.fr

Netherlands
Dekker Pepper dekkerpepper.nl
Heatsupply heatsupply.nl

Belgium
The Chilli Shop EU thechillishop.eu
chilisaus.be

Denmark
Chili Klaus chiliklaus.dk – also a brilliant
YouTube star too!

Switzerland
Dr HotSauce's Spicy World
hotsauce.ch/en

Japan
Hot Sauce Bar
hot-sauce-bar.myshopify.com

Africa
The Sauce Shop thesauceshop.co.za

Philippines
Original Hot Sauce Store
originalhotsaucestore.com

Australia

Blonde Chilli blondechilli.com.au
ChilliBOM chillibom.com.au
Culley's culleys.co.nz
Mat's Hot Shop matshotshop.com
Sauce Mania saucemania.com.au
The Chilli Shop Kuranda
thechillishopkuranda.com.au

Hot Sauce Related Events

US/Canada

bostonhotsaucefest.com
(Boston, Massachusetts)
buffalowing.com (Buffalo, New York)
fieryfoodsshow.com
(Albuquerque, New Mexico)
hatchchilefest.com
(Hatch, New Mexico)
heatingupthecapital.ca (Ontario,
Canada)
heatwaveexpo.com (London, Ontario,
Canada)
ilikeithotfestival.com (Largo, Florida)
indianahotluck.us (Madison, Indiana)
newenglandhotsaucefest.com
(Hampton, New Hampshire)
nychotsauceexpo.com (New York)
oldboneymtnhotsummernight.com
(Thousand Oaks, California)
pdxhotsauceexpo.com (Portland,
Oregon)
pueblochilefestival.com
(Pueblo, Colorado)
saucetoberfest.com
(Flemington, New Jersey)
texashotsaucefestival.com
(Houston, Texas)
zestfest.net (Dallas, Texas)

Europe

berlinchilifest.com (Berlin, Germany)
detente/fete-piment.php
(Espelette, France)
dutchchilifest.nl (Eindhoven, Netherlands)
espelette-paysbasque.com (Espelette,
France)
fieramondialedelpeperoncino.com (Rieti,
Italy)
greatdorsetchillifestival.co.uk
(Dorset, UK)
hotsaucesociety.co.uk
(Birmingham and London, UK)
meatopia.co.uk (London, UK)

Rest of World

**joylab.co.nz/sweat-shop/hot-sauce-
festival** (Auckland, New Zealand)
**welcometobrunswick.com.au/hot-sauce-
and-chilli-fest** (Melbourne, Australia)

Books and Websites

An Anarchy of Chillies by Caz Hildebrand
Favourite Spice by Kay Plunkett-Hogge
Fermented Hot Sauce Cookbook
by Kristen Wood
*Heat: Cooking with Chillies, the World's
Peppers of the Americas*
by Maricel E. Presilla
The Hot Sauce Cookbook by Robb Walsh
101 Chillies to Try Before You Die
by David Floyd

chili-plant.com
chilipeppermadness.com
cliftonchilliclub.com
crafthotsauce.com
dochotties.com
pepperscale.com

ACKNOWLEDGEMENTS

We'd like to issue huge, sizzling-hot hugs to the following friends, sauce-meisters and loved ones, without whom this book wouldn't have happened:

Martine Carter, our awesome agent at Sauce Management, Stacey Cleworth, Emily Lapworth, Katy Everett and all at Quadrille, Naomi Wilkinson for the illustrations, Frank Jay at the brilliant Leeds Chilli Shop, Andy Bibey, Luca Rollini, Alex Khoo (for his beef ribs recipe), Liam Kirwan, Liam Kerr, Yoyo Xayavongchanch, Allie at Hot Sauce Society, Brooklyn and Alex at Hunter PR, Took Osborn, Erica Diehl, Freek Raijmakers, King Phojanakong, Dan Fitzgerald, Clint Meyer, Rob Fletcher, Kate O'Neil, Stephen Notman, Chris Papple, Joel Harrison and, finally, our families – Carrie, Lois and Honor, and Philippa, Orson and Hal – for not complaining too much about the lack of shelf space in our fridges and being robust guinea pigs for the hundreds of sauces we made you try.

ABOUT THE AUTHORS

Neil Ridley is an award-winning writer, broadcaster and consultant in the world of food and drink. He has co-written six books about spirits, cocktails and drinks culture, including *Distilled* (now published in 14 languages), *The World Atlas of Gin*, *The World of Whisky*, *Straight Up* and *60-Second Cocktails*.

He also has life-long passions for electronic music (having previously worked as a record executive for Warner Bros Records) and the culture of hot sauce, which led him to a great friendship with his writing partner Dean.

Dean Honer is an award-winning musician and record producer (I Monster/The All Seeing I/The Moonlandingz/The Human League) who has spent the last 25 years touring the globe and recording over a dozen albums.

An eventful trip to Austin, Texas, which included supporting Iggy Pop and eating some amazing Mexican street food, was an eye-opening, palate-burning revelation that exposed him to a huge variety of hot sauce. The rest of the tour was spent exploring the taco trucks, sauce shops and farmers' markets in search of the perfect hot sauce and the hottest chillies.

Managing Director Sarah Lavelle
Commissioning Editor Stacey Cleworth
Designer Katy Everett
Illustrator Naomi Wilkinson
Head of Production Stephen Lang
Senior Production Controller Katie Jarvis

Published in 2023 by Quadrille
an imprint of Hardie Grant Publishing

Quadrille
52–54 Southwark Street
London SE1 1UN
quadrille.com

Cataloguing in Publication Data: a catalogue record for this book is available from the
British Library.

ISBN 9781837830626

Printed in China

MIX
Paper | Supporting
responsible forestry
FSC™ C020056